TEACHING English Language Learners K-12

A Quick-Start Guide for the New Teacher

JERRY JESNESS

TEACHING English Language Learners K-12

A Quick-Start Guide for the New Teacher

Foreword by Rosalie Pedalino Porter

CORWIN PRESS
A Sage Publications Company
Thousand Oaks, California

For information:

Corwin Press
A Sage Publications Company
2455 Teller Road
Thousand Oaks, California 91320
www.corwinpress.com

Sage Publications Ltd.
1 Oliver's Yard
55 City Road
London EC1Y 1SP
United Kingdom

Sage Publications India Pvt. Ltd.
B-42, Panchsheel Enclave
Post Box 4109
New Delhi 110 017 India

Printed in the United States of America

Library of Congress Cataloging-in-Publication Data

Jesness, Jerry.
Teaching English language learners K-12 : a quick-start guide for the new teacher / by Jerry Jesness.
        p. cm.
Includes bibliographical references (p.) and index.
ISBN 0-7619-3186-4 (Cloth) — ISBN 0-7619-3187-2 (Paper)
    1. English language—Study and teaching—Foreign speakers. I. Title.
PE1128.A2J47 2004
428'.0071'2—dc22

                                                2003019020

This book is printed on acid-free paper.

    05   06   07   08   10 9 8 7 6 5 4 3 2

Acquisitions Editor:	Faye Zucker
Editorial Assistant:	Stacy Wagner
Typesetter:	C&M Digitals (P) Ltd.
Indexer:	Sheila Bodell
Cover Designer:	Tracy E. Miller
Production Artist:	Katherine Minerva

Contents

26 06

118173

Foreword

Jerry Jesness's *Teaching English Language Learners K–12: A Quick-Start Guide for the New Teacher* fills a crucial need in the education of a growing number of children who enter U.S. public schools with little or no knowledge of the English language. Four and a half million children, now described officially as English Language Learners, are enrolled in schools across the country, with the greatest concentration in California, where one of every five students fits this description. Before highlighting the particular strengths of this *Guide* for teachers and administrators, it is useful to explain why the information conveyed in this volume is so important at this time.

The field of English as a Second Language (ESL) teaching has evolved and improved dramatically over the past 35 years. Following the state and federal laws and a U.S. Supreme Court decision *requiring* special help for English Language Learners, enormous activity has been expended in producing effective models, teaching strategies, and materials for helping children of all ages gain mastery of the English language for access to an equal educational opportunity. However, since most of the emphasis has been on bilingual education programs based on native-language teaching, the ESL component played a minor role. Most of the effort in colleges of education across the country has endorsed the gradual, transitional nature of bilingual programs, the slow shift from learning in the native language to learning in English, with less emphasis on English language and literacy as the prime goal.

This *Quick-Start Guide* fills another hole in the ESL field by focusing not only on young learners but on the urgent needs of older students in grades 4–12. Although these older students make up about one-third of all English Language Learners, their needs are much more pressing as they have fewer years ahead in school and they must meet much more challenging academic standards than their younger classmates if they are to master the language, literacy, and course content for high school graduation. Most attention in the publishing field has, naturally enough, been given to the education of younger English Language Learners who enter school in kindergarten through grade 3, and this *Guide* does provide good, practical ideas for teachers in the primary grades.

Two other factors affect the timeliness of the *Quick-Start Guide*: the high standards, high-stakes testing movement across the states, and the swelling sea of change in state laws, away from a focus on native-language teaching in favor of expanded ESL, usually called "English Immersion." Two-thirds of the states now require a tenth-grade test to be passed for high school graduation, generally a test of English literacy and mathematics, and these mandates are further supported by the federal requirements of the No Child Left Behind policy. English Language Learners are held accountable for meeting the same standards as their native English-speaking classmates, a daunting prospect for many. The changes in state education laws in California (1998), Arizona (2000), and Massachusetts (2002) now require students of non-English background to be provided an intensive English learning program from the first day of school, with the clear objective of rapid and effective language, literacy, and subject matter learning in English. This expansion of the role of English as a Second Language teaching calls for recruiting and training (or retraining) of teachers on a large scale. For this, the *Quick-Start Guide* is an excellent primary resource.

The valuable classroom experience in the author's background and a genuine sensitivity for his students' needs are evident on every page of clear prose. How I would have benefited from having a guide of this sort in the decade when I directed the Bilingual/ESL programs for the Newton Public Schools in Massachusetts from 1980 to 1990! The practical information included here addresses the major issues in educating language minority students, without overloading the new teacher with extraneous matter. Among the basic ideas examined with sufficient thoroughness:

- The enormous variety in student backgrounds (first language, previous education or the lack thereof, socioeconomic status, family mobility) that poses great challenges for teachers in setting realistic goals, instructional grouping, pacing of lessons, and testing.
- The age-old question of introducing the different aspects of language, i.e., focus on speaking and listening comprehension first and for how long? when to introduce reading, writing? how much to focus on grammar, vocabulary, error correction, and spelling? when to initiate subject matter learning in English and how (with a few useful examples in science and social studies given)?
- A discussion of grading policies for students from such disparate backgrounds, as well as evaluating when English Language Learners are best prepared to work independently in mainstream classrooms, for part or all of the school day.
- The dilemma of distinguishing between students with learning disabilities and students acquiring a second language—sound advice for avoiding the misclassification of English Language Learners as learning disabled.

- A good review of appropriate teaching materials, especially in the area of computer assisted learning, a set of reproducible lessons for beginner students in the classroom, and a section on professional resources and organizations.

This book delivers what it promises—a concise array of teaching strategies, curriculum, and things ESL teachers need to know to become most confident in their work and most effective with their students. Truly important lessons for readers are present throughout the book: These students deserve the encouragement and support of the entire school community and are not just the responsibility of the ESL teacher alone; and given the essential learning opportunities we provide, English Language Learners are capable of high achievement in our schools and in our society as future productive, self-fulfilled adults.

Rosalie Pedalino Porter, Ed.D.
Amherst, Massachusetts

Preface

This is an exciting time to be teaching English as a second language. Events of the past few years have made it clear that immigrants and hyphenated Americans want their children to speak English and to speak it well. The standards movement is drawing attention to the importance of academic performance for all ethnic groups. There is a genuine realization that all students can and should learn.

When I began teaching English as a second language in Texas two decades ago, I often heard the comments, "It takes three generations to educate these people," and "Once a LEP [a student with limited English proficiency], always a LEP." I have not heard either comment lately. One hopes those dark days are gone.

Clearly the mastery of English is not negotiable. Pressure is increasing to improve both English-language education and the English-language component of bilingual education. The demands made on teachers of English as a second language are great. In many states these tasks fall to teachers who have had little preparation. Some states require only a few college classes for an ESL endorsement, and some certify teachers to teach English as a second language based only on inservice training. Many states allow out-of-field teachers to teach ESL or offer emergency credentials to teachers who have language teaching training that is short of what is normally required. Teachers of mathematics, social studies, or science who have had no training in language teaching whatsoever may have non-English-speaking students placed in their classes. Because you have picked up a book that professes to be a quick-start guide for teachers of English learners, chances are you are or will soon become one such teacher.

Like the blind men who felt and then described an elephant, a novice teacher may fixate on just a few aspects of language. English is no more a mere collection of grammatical rules than an elephant is just its trunk. It is no more just the written word than the elephant is just its tail. This book will deal with all key aspects of language.

This book will also deal with some of the realities of language learning that are sometimes avoided in textbooks. If you are in a typical public school ESL situation, you will teach some students who have attended little school in their native countries. You will sooner or later encounter peers and superiors who want to use your program as a tool of segregation. You will deal with those who confuse incomplete mastery of English with learning disabilities or lack of intelligence. These are challenging but not insurmountable problems. Forewarned is forearmed. This book will help you negotiate these situations.

In many ways, ESL teachers can feel intellectually isolated. Teachers and administrators who have not been trained to teach math or science at least have studied those subjects. The United States is not a nation of language learners, so a great many of your peers and superiors, and perhaps you yourself, lack the experience of successfully learning a second language. Sometimes explaining what you are doing to those who have neither taught nor learned languages is like trying to describe colors to the blind.

Although this book is written primarily for the novice teacher of the English language, it is my hope that experienced teachers will also read it, not as a guidebook, and certainly not as a quick-start manual, but rather as one side of a conversation with another old hand. It might have a few new ideas that an experienced teacher will want to consider, or it may be worthwhile just to read about what worked in another teacher's classroom. Or an experienced teacher might use this book as a tool to help educate fellow teachers and superiors about some of the realities that ESL teachers face.

Acknowledgments

I would like to thank my editors, Faye Zucker, Stacy Wagner, and Rachel Livsey, as well as educator/author Elaine McEwan, who introduced me to Corwin Press. A special thank you goes to Elizabeth Anne Jesness, my wife and best friend, for her love and support while I wrote this book.

Corwin Press extends its thanks to the following reviewers for their contributions to this book:

Barbara Foulks Boyd, Radford University, Radford, Virginia

Rachael Hungerford, Lycoming College, Williamsport, Pennsylvania

María Elena Reyes, University of Alaska Fairbanks, Fairbanks, Alaska

About the Author

In Jerry Jesness's 25-year career as an educator, he has worked with English learners in a number of environments. He has taught ESL in public middle and high schools, special education for bilingual children at the elementary level, and language arts and social studies in classes that included both English learners and regular education students. Jesness has also taught students privately, ranging from preschoolers to top executives of multinational corporations. Over the years, he has worked for the Bureau of Indian Affairs, for public schools near the Texas-Mexico border, for Berlitz Language Schools, and for small, privately owned language schools in Mexico and Japan.

Jesness holds a BA in English from the University of Minnesota, Morris, and he earned an MA in Spanish and an ESL teaching endorsement from the University of Texas, Pan American. He was the first non-Hispanic to earn a graduate degree in Spanish literature from UT Pan American. Jesness currently lives in Harlingen, Texas, with his wife and three daughters, and he teaches at Los Fresnos High School. His email address is *furnes@yahoo.com.* You may also visit his Web site at *www.jesness.com.*

1

The Joys and Challenges of Teaching English

THE JOYS OF TEACHING ESL

If you are or will be teaching English as a second language, you are in many ways fortunate. Unlike many teachers, you have a genuine mandate to teach a real academic subject, a language, and to teach it well. Teachers who have a serious academic bent sometimes complain that they feel pressured to teach with the brakes on. You, on the other hand, as an ESL teacher, are expected to help students master a new language, prepare them to study academic subjects in that language, and help them adjust to a new culture. While some foreign language teachers complain that they are neither allowed sufficient time nor given a serious mandate to impart their subject, you will have both.

Your students will be more motivated than most, or at least they can be if you figure out how to reach them. With very few exceptions, your students want to know English. Unlike students of foreign languages who might never have the opportunity to use their new language outside the classroom, your students will likely use their new language every day. For them, English is a living subject that they can put to use on a daily basis. Those who are not interested in knowing English on the first day of class will soon change their minds. After just a few months of living in the United States, the advantages of knowing English and the disadvantages of not being able to communicate in the prevailing local language become obvious.

Very few of my students were actually hostile to knowing English. Only two readily come to mind. One was a student who was sent to live with relatives in Texas after being expelled from middle school in Mexico and was trying to get expelled from our school as well. The other was a teenaged girl who was determined to do nothing that would please her English-speaking stepmother, although her brother was one of my most motivated students.

Some of your students will, of course, be more interested than others. Not all of your students will have sufficient intrinsic motivation to learn as much English as you want them to know. It is, of course, part of your job to bring them a motivating spark. But the fact that your students at least want to know that which you have to teach gives you an advantage that not all teachers enjoy.

Travel the World With or Without Leaving Your Classroom

If your taste runs to the exotic, English teaching offers you opportunities not available to the average teacher. ESL teachers are in demand throughout the world. You will need a bit of luck or maybe the right friends to land one of the plum jobs in a high-paying school for the children of embassy staff or wealthy businesspeople or in a prep school for young people planning to study at a university in an English-speaking country, but it will be easy to find a humbler, lower-paying job that offers the opportunity to live and work in a country that you have always dreamed of visiting.

Even if you never leave your native country, English teaching offers the opportunity to have some interesting experiences. You will get to know some fascinating people, both your students and those of their community, and you will likely get a chance to experience parts of their culture more deeply than do most "outsiders." Other teachers occasionally receive an apple from a student; we ESL teachers receive mangos, sushi, tamales, kim-chi, saltenos, chapatis, and wojapi, both literally and figuratively.

THE CHALLENGES OF TEACHING ESL

It has been said that learning a language is like drinking water from a fire hose. Before becoming able to communicate in a second language, learners must learn literally thousands of new words. To attain a level of fluency equivalent to that of educated native speakers, they must learn more than one hundred thousand. They must work with a phonological system that includes sounds that they may not initially even be able to distinguish, much less pronounce. They must not only learn but also assimilate and become able to automatically apply new syntactical rules. In addition to the teaching of the language itself, English teaching in public schools brings a special set of challenges.

Unlike students at private schools that offer intensive language study, your students will probably be expected to make progress in all required academic subjects. Whereas English and content classes can enhance one another, the dual tasks of learning a new language while advancing in math, science, and social studies are demanding indeed. The lot of the English learner is somewhat like that of a student who takes on a full academic load while participating in a dozen extracurricular activities.

There are, alas, those who see ESL as some sort of a remedial class. Quite frankly, some people view those with whom they cannot communicate as feebleminded. Of course, to those who do not understand our language, we seem pretty dim as well. The reality is that, if your students are to succeed, ESL must be one of the most demanding classes offered at your school. Any teacher who treats ESL as "academics light" is doomed to fail. Never forget, nor let your peers forget, that English learners are as able as any students in your school, and that your ESL class is and must be a demanding one. Language learning is not for sissies, and neither is language teaching.

It's More Than a Job, It's a Mission

For your students, language learning is more than important, it is essential. Although there are a few people who manage to make a comfortable living in the United States without ever having mastered English, the odds are against those who do not speak the language of the land. Then there are people who manage to learn English after a decade or so but, as a result of years of not understanding their teachers, missed out on much of their education. Such students drop out of school able to speak English but without the skills required of a high school graduate. On the other hand, opportunities galore exist for bilingual individuals who possess a solid education. Your class is the critical transitional step into the English part of that education.

2

Your Students

Depending on where you teach, you may or may not have great ethnic and linguistic variety in your classes. If you teach in an ethnically diverse part of a metropolitan area, in a suburban school that serves a varied community of businesspeople and professionals, or in a boarding school that serves many foreign students, the composition of your class may resemble the United Nations. If you teach in a border community, a rural area where most immigrants came to work in a specific industry, in an urban ethnic enclave, or in a community that has recently welcomed a refugee population, chances are that most of your students will speak the same language. Each situation offers its own advantages and challenges. When all students speak the same language, you can note similarities and differences between their language and English and adjust instruction accordingly. If your class resembles the Tower of Babel, you will lack this advantage, but you have another. In such a class, English will be the only possible medium of communication among your students, a situation that will oblige them to use English frequently both in and out of your class.

Do not assume that you will be teaching a homogeneous group of students even if all of your students come from the same country. Your students will likely be a diverse mix of rich, middle-class, and poor, urban, suburban, and rural students hailing from deserts, prairies, mountains, and coastal plains.

If you teach in a secondary school, you will likely have a number of students who have not attended as many years of school as their age would indicate. Many countries do not have compulsory education laws like those in the United States. Mexico, the homeland of the largest number of new immigrants in the United States, requires students to attend school only through *secundaria,* the equivalent of our junior high school. Compulsory education laws in Mexico, however, are not always strictly enforced, and some isolated rural communities are served only by elementary schools or are not served by any schools at all.

In some states, English learners are placed according to age regardless of their prior education. It is not uncommon for high school ESL classes to include students who attended prep schools mixed with students who have attended only a few years of elementary school. This mix presents special challenges for ESL teachers. These challenges will be discussed in various chapters of this book.

The definition of English learner is not as simple as it seems. It is obvious that the recent immigrant who responds to your cheery "Good morning" with a blank stare lacks English proficiency. With children who have grown up with two languages, or with those who have been in bilingual or ESL programs for some time and have mastered most but not all English language skills, or with those who seem to have mastered oral English but lack basic academic skills, the line is not always clear.

ESL, ELL, LEP, AND OTHER ACRONYMS

You probably teach or will teach in a BE (bilingual education) or an ESL (English as a second language) program. ESL is also know as ESOL (English for speakers of other languages), EFL (English as a foreign language), and EAL (English as another language). English learners are identified by a number of acronyms. Your students will be identified either as ELL (English language learners) or LEP (limited English proficient) students, depending on the state in which you teach. They will also be labeled according to the level of their mastery of English, perhaps as NES (non-English speaker) or NFES (non-fluent English speaker) or even FES/NER/NEW (fluent English speaker/non-English reader/non-English writer), or perhaps their level will be indicated by an acronym followed by a number. Some teachers believe that English language education suffers from ENCA (excess number of confusing acronyms). To the greatest extent possible, this book will eschew acronyms and refer to ELL/LEP/ESOL/NES/NFES students simply as *English learners.*

PLACEMENT IN BILINGUAL AND ESL PROGRAMS

The process of placement in and exit from bilingual and ESL programs and classification within the programs is extremely important. In some states, like Texas, these tasks fall to a campus committee. In Texas the committee is called the Language Placement Assessment Committee, or LPAC. This committee considers such data as test scores, classroom performance, and parent information.

Some states like California mandate that placement and reclassification decisions be made locally but do not specify exactly who should make the decision. Some California districts have committees similar to the Texas LPAC, while others allow these decisions to be made by the teacher, an administrator, and the students' parents.

In all states the process will begin with a home language survey. The parents will declare which language the child speaks at home. If that language is not English, the student will be tested. For very young children, only an oral English test will be administered. Older students will be given tests of both oral and written English and perhaps basic skills tests as well. Most students will be tested in their native language as well as in English.

Testing procedures vary from state to state. Some states have their own test, like the California English Language Development Test, or CELDT, while others allow schools to choose from a list of approved tests.

It is important that the testing be done well. It is especially easy to err with the oral language test. Someone who does not understand how to interpret the results of an oral language test might misinterpret poor listening comprehension skills that result from a short attention span as an inability to understand English, so it is important for the examiner to be trained in the use of the testing instrument. Even the most competent examiners, however, can occasionally misclassify a student. Shy students may test poorly simply because they do not feel comfortable speaking with the examiner. If a student tests out as a nonspeaker or limited speaker of both English and his or her home language, assume that something is amiss and retest. If a shy student who has been mistakenly labeled a non-English speaker proves able to speak English reasonably well in nontesting situations, call a meeting if necessary and arrange to retest and change to the appropriate classification.

SEP STUDENTS (SOMEONE ELSE'S PROBLEM)

In his science fiction spoof, *The Hitchhiker's Guide to the Galaxy,* author Douglas Adams explains that it is impossible to make an object truly invisible, but that if an object is deemed somebody else's problem, nobody will notice it. An advanced alien civilization applied this principle to the development of an SEP (someone else's problem) ray, which creates a force field that makes an object appear to be someone else's problem, thus rendering it effectively invisible. Be forewarned that there could be unscrupulous individuals who will use the identification process to take difficult English-dominant students out of regular classes and place them in yours. An LEP or ELL classification is a handy way for an influential but unethical teacher to move a difficult student from his or her class. In some states, such misclassification can buy a test exemption for an academically weak student. Misclassification of English learners is most likely to happen when the ESL teacher is new on the job. By making these students someone else's problem (yours), they make them invisible, preventing them from getting the services they need to succeed. For the students' sake, do not tolerate such an abuse of the system.

INCLUSION AND SUPPORT IN REGULAR CLASSROOMS

Depending on your state's rules and the individual student, some of your students may be in a bilingual or English as a second language program for several years. Clearly it is not appropriate to place students in their fourth year in American schools in the same class as those who just entered the country. Recent immigrants will need a heavy dose of oral language, while fourth- or fifth-year students may speak English fluently but remain in the program because they are still weak in English literacy skills. This sort of placement does, however, sometimes happen. If the population of English learners at your school is small, you may be the only ESL teacher for students at various stages of language learning. This does not mean that all English learners should spend all of their time in your class. After one year at the very most, English learners will benefit if they spend at least part of their school day among native speakers of English. In some cases, depending on your state's laws and your students' skills, it may be appropriate for an advanced but not yet exited English learner to spend the entire academic day in regular classes with the ESL teacher providing support. The same people who make placement and exit decisions can help make decisions about inclusion and support for English learners in regular classes. There will be more about English learners in regular classes in Chapter 15.

3

Your Toolbox

Teachers of ESL will have a textbook and probably a curriculum guide, but they will not have the luxury of following them lockstep. Given the range of motivation, ability, and prior education found in most ESL classes, most teachers will have to work on more than one track and will need materials and equipment that will enable them to do so.

MATERIALS AND EQUIPMENT

The Textbook

When choosing your textbook, it is essential to consider what your students do outside of your classroom. If they spend much time in the mainstream or in sheltered English content classes, they will need less vocabulary from you than would students who are studying other academic subjects in their native language. Those who have many opportunities to speak English outside your class will need less listening and speaking activities than those whose real-world contact with English is limited.

You will also need to consider how much your students are expected to learn. A surprising number of schools do not take this into consideration. If students are expected to enter the mainstream, even with support, after a single year, a textbook that covers a mere 1,000-word vocabulary will not be sufficient. The words *First Year Course* in the title do not necessarily mean that the book is appropriate for an entire year in your class. Some such books are indeed intended for a full year of study, but in a class that meets only two or three hours per week. Teachers whose classes meet for three or four hours daily will find that such a book covers enough material only for a month or two.

Some books are long on structure but short on vocabulary, or vice versa. A textbook might cover such difficult structures as the past conditional yet contain vocabulary of only 1,000 or 2,000 words. This is not in and of itself a weakness, but such books should be supplemented.

Other Books

A supplemental reader will be especially valuable for those whose textbooks are vocabulary poor. It is also a good idea to have a library of books on various subjects for the students to check out. For students who are competent readers of another language, bilingual dictionaries are a must. For others, have unilingual English dictionaries of various levels of difficulty.

Realia: Pictures, Maps, Charts, Toys, and More

If you are teaching beginning speakers of English, have a large box full of props. Beginning students best learn vocabulary when they see or, better yet, handle an object as they learn its name. Toys work well, even with adults. The genuine article is the best when practical, but toys are usually cheaper and more compact. A large, well-furnished doll house is most useful. A large collection of pictures, maps, and charts is also a must.

Audio Tapes and CDs

Because listening is the first and arguably the most important language skill, have a variety of taped materials for your students. Many textbooks come with tapes or CDs. If possible, get one set for each student. If not, at least have some classroom sets available both to use in class and to check out. Taped books at various levels of difficulty are also useful.

Gadgets Galore

Technology has been a great boon to language teachers. At one time language laboratories were luxuries and video equipment was beyond the reach of schools. Now, language-teaching technology is a bargain. A $500 computer can now do what expensive language labs used to do, and much more. Some programs allow computers to do much of what could once be done only with a one-on-one tutor. Personal Digital Assistants (PDAs), both Palm devices and Pocket PCs, allow learners easy portable access to both the written and the spoken word. The lowly tape recorder is also a great boon to language learners. Portable tape and disc players now allow students to practice their language lessons as they jog, lift weights, wait for the bus, or clean their rooms. For in-class use, a few $35 tape recorders with several headphones each can serve as listening stations.

Some good English courses are available on videotape. Even if you do not use them with your entire class, you might choose to do so with students who get behind or need to review key concepts. Movies on videotape can also be valuable language learning tools. A video camera and a VCR can help students keep track of their own progress.

PAYING FOR YOUR TOOLS

Veteran teachers eventually manage to purchase, collect, and hoard most of the equipment and materials they need, but getting the right equipment can be difficult for those just starting out. Seek materials and equipment where you can. When businesses or classes upgrade their computers, they might be willing to give you their old ones. The older Pentium 2 and Mac Quadra may be adequate for your purposes. Libraries may have material that they can donate. Co-workers might be willing to donate toys that their children have outgrown for your realia collection, and students may have items that they are willing to either donate or lend.

Keep your eyes open for available funding. After months or even years of scraping by on a starvation budget, you may discover that lavish funds seem to appear out of thin air. Sometimes budgets for ESL classes increase phenomenally after visits from advocacy groups or state agencies. One year after such a visit, my classes were moved from a crowded attic above the bilingual office to a spacious, air-conditioned classroom complete with networked computers.

Although funding will vary, some will usually be available every year. Use your program's money wisely and you will eventually have all that you need. Bear in mind, however, that every veteran teacher's closet is a graveyard of failed innovations, so purchase wisely.

GETTING HELP FROM VOLUNTEERS

The best way to learn a language is by speaking it. If possible, English learners should have every opportunity to practice what they learn in class. Unless your classes are tiny, you should seek volunteers to engage your students in conversation. If the school has study halls or designated activity time, English-speaking students can be recruited to help. Some schools have future-teacher organizations that may contribute volunteers. If there is a university nearby, education students can be recruited. Clergymen usually know of people who are willing to volunteer time. Senior citizen groups, civic groups, and organizations for retired people may also be helpful.

GETTING ADVICE AND HELP
FROM SCHOOL PERSONNEL

Ideally, you will have around you teachers and administrators with experience successfully teaching English learners. If your district lacks personnel with training and experience in the field, seek help where you can get it. Of course, you will have access to the usual support staff: principals, counselors, facilitators, and the like, but other staff members may be able to provide valuable advice as well. If any school in your district offers classes in your students' language as a foreign language, then you might find some help in the foreign language department. If you do not speak the students' language, a teacher of that language can help you understand differences and similarities with English. Teachers who have spent time in your students' native country or have studied its history and literature can help you with cultural issues. Although you will not want to run your class exactly like a foreign language class, foreign language teachers can share some ideas and techniques that will work with your students.

Speech therapists can also offer good advice. Therapists know points of articulation and understand other factors involved in producing sounds. A therapist who speaks your students' language or who has done quite a bit of work with native speakers of your students' language can explain similarities and differences with English. Therapists are trained to teach developmental language, which includes vocabulary development and improvement in language usage. You will not, of course, want your English class to mirror speech therapy, but speech therapists can offer you some valuable insights and ideas. Your co-workers realize that your job is a big one, and most will be happy to help you out.

4

How Much? How Soon? How Fast?

How long should it take to learn English? There is no simple answer to this question. How long does it take to learn to play chess or the French horn? It depends on the individual. Of course, there will be great variance between students. Talent and motivation for language learning vary greatly, as do opportunities to practice. Still, you will need one or several timelines.

BICS AND CALP

University of Toronto professor Jim Cummins invented and popularized the acronyms BICS (basic interpersonal communication skills) and CALP (cognitive academic learning proficiencies). By Cummins's reckoning, it should take a learner at least two years to achieve BICS—that is, enough English to communicate effectively in social situations—but at least five years to master CALP—sufficient academic skills to compete in English language classes with native speakers.

Cummins stresses that CALP transfers from one language to another. If you are teaching upper elementary or secondary levels, most of your students will have academic skills in their native languages. Some will likely have academic skills that match or exceed those of the native speakers in your school's gifted and talented program. I have found that students who have attended *escuela preparatoria*, the Mexican equivalent of high school, are much more knowledgeable and have stronger academic skills than the typical American high school student. To be fair to my compatriots, let it be noted that most American students attend high school and only a minority of Mexican students attend *preparatoria*, so this is not a truly equitable comparison.

If you are teaching secondary school you will likely have several students who have not attended as much school as their age would indicate. In many states, such students are placed in ESL classes based on their age rather than on their academic record. You will also probably someday have some students who have never attended school anywhere. Because these students have few academic skills in any language, they will require more time, probably several years more, to master English CALP.

It is true that most English learners will score below national norms on standardized tests during their first few years of English study. Still, for English learners who are at or near grade level in their native language, five years to CALP seems longer than it needs to be, unless we define CALP as a command of English equal to that of an educated native speaker. Again, many academic skills will transfer from the native language. Although one needs a decent command of English for academic study, absolute mastery is not necessary. Many students with decent, albeit limited, English do quite well in regular classes even though their written work may contain some errors. A great many valedictorian speeches have been delivered in flawed English.

Most students should be able to attain BICS in one year and CALP in three, assuming that they have the latter skills in their native language. Although the research on BICS and CALP points to a timetable to mastery as wide-ranging as one to seven years, and a fuller discussion of the topic could easily fill an entire book, this is my goal for students. I must admit that some of my students have failed to meet this goal. Given human nature, not all students will give their best effort, and not all bilingual and ESL programs will be as good as they should be. Some students may drag their feet for a year or two before getting serious about their English studies. Materials may not be adequate for the diverse students in an ESL class. Some languages differ more from English than others. Speakers of languages with many English cognates and parallel grammatical structures will find English easier to learn than those whose native languages bear little similarity to English. Those who require more than one year to master BICS and three for CALP should be forgiven, especially those who are learning disabled or who attended little school before immigrating. Having large numbers of students spending more than three years mastering English should, however, raise a red flag, and students who are not on track to meet these goals should be targeted for extra help.

PIE-IN-THE-SKY GOALS

One of the greatest frustrations we ESL teachers face is dealing with planners who set pie-in-the-sky goals and then ignore them. I once taught in a program that professed to prepare Southeast Asian students to succeed in American university or technical school classes after only nine months of language study. To my knowledge, none of our students met that ambitious goal, and some students repeated the course as many as five times. In one middle school, my pleas to establish a timetable that included partial inclusion after the first semester and ESL classes and support for a total of three years fell on deaf ears. At the planning stage, we were supposed to make our students fluent in one year. After all, we must have high expectations. When at the end of the year few students had met this ambitious and unrealistic goal, we had the usual excuses: These kids are poor and disadvantaged. They come from slums and goat farms. The result was that many students repeated beginning ESL. I recall that one of the administration's champions of high standards chastised me for giving my students 75 to 100 vocabulary and spelling words per week. She suggested that I lower the number to 15, a pace that would enable my middle school students to write English reasonably well by the age of 40.

Know the truth, and the truth will set you free. If the stated standards are not being met, change either the standards or the program. If the standards are unreasonable, change them. If they are reasonable but are not being met, improve the program.

IS ONE YEAR ENOUGH?

At the time of this writing, the voters of at least two states had faced referendums to limit English instruction to a single year. One year is cutting it pretty short. It is ironic that a nation that sometimes tolerates university professors of foreign languages who have limited command of the languages they teach would demand that children master a language in so little time. I suspect that the one-year goal may have been an overreaction to a system that had left many students with limited English skills after five or more years of study.

This is not to say that there are no students who can learn English in a single year. Some, but not all, very young students master new languages very quickly. Among older learners, linguistic prodigies do exist. Once in my career I recommended that a middle school student exit from my class and enter all-English classes for the gifted after only one semester. Although she did not yet possess full native fluency, she could carry on a reasonably intelligent conversation in English and had superb academic skills in her native Spanish. She was able to handle grade-level academic work in English with the aid of a bilingual dictionary, and she was willing to take the time necessary to do so. She was not, of course, a typical student. I have also had a handful of students who were ready to fully enter the mainstream and succeed there with only minimal support after only a year. All of these students still had deficits in their English and would have benefited from after-school tutoring sessions with ESL specialists. For students of average ability, however, mastery of English in three years is a reasonable goal.

Do not be surprised if, at the end of three years of language instruction, even your best students' English is still a bit flawed. There will likely be some errors in the use of difficult structures and prepositions, and vocabulary will likely be weaker than that of native speakers. The students as a group will likely score lower on English reading and writing tests than their native-speaker peers for a few more years. Do not let this discourage you or your students. Students who test out at the thirtieth percentile in one language and at the seventieth in another need not feel inferior to students who test at the ninetieth percentile in the only language that they know. Students with flawed English can achieve much in the mainstream, especially if they use their equalizers, their dictionaries.

WHEN SHOULD STUDENTS EXIT TO REGULAR CLASSES?

The CALP argument is sometimes used to keep students out of the mainstream longer than necessary. Many students who possess oral English BICS and rudimentary English writing skills can do quite well in the mainstream for at least part of the day. One does not need to speak English perfectly in order to study successfully among native speakers. Just think about your university classmates. Some of the most successful were foreign students who spoke imperfect English. We have heard about the disadvantages of sink-or-swim language immersion. At least as bad, however, is stay-out-of-the-water-until-you-are-sure-you-can-swim segregation. Your students should spend some time in classes with native speakers as soon as they know enough English to make some sense of what is going on there. There will be more on this subject in Chapter 15.

STEEP HILLS AND FRUSTRATING PLATEAUS

Do not be discouraged by what appears to be lack of progress. Often bits of knowledge build up in the language learner's mind, link themselves together, and then later manifest themselves in chunks. This is true of all language skills. The student who could not pronounce a single English word intelligibly might, after months of seemingly pointless practice, appear to master half a dozen sounds all at once. One who could not produce a grammatical sentence a few days ago might suddenly start using several structures correctly, and one who failed every vocabulary test in the first semester might start correctly using words that were studied and seemingly not learned months before. One who could not spell more than a handful of words even after months of practice might grasp a dozen rules of English spelling at once. Just when you start to feel like a sculptor who has been trying to carve granite with a butter knife, you will see students rise to new levels.

When students reach a new level, they fill with pride. Once they become comfortable with their new skills, however, they will see the next level and become frustrated that they have not arrived there yet. Beginning language learners are delighted the first time an English utterance is understood. Soon they will not be content with utterances but will want to join in conversations. Once conversant, they may feel frustration at the inability to give a formal speech in English. A reader who was once delighted to read warning signs may some day be frustrated at an inability to understand James Joyce or William Faulkner, a frustration that most of us native speakers of English share. As a teacher, you can use this cycle of pride, comfort, frustration, and pride again to keep your students moving forward.

You can help assuage feelings of frustration with video clips. You can videotape your students at different stages of their language development. When they start feeling that their progress is inadequate, show them clips of themselves struggling with a concept that they have since mastered.

MOTIVATION INSIDE AND OUTSIDE OF CLASS

Motivation figures heavily into the formula. As teachers, it is our job to make our subject as interesting as possible. Some motivating factors are, however, out of our hands. When students find English personally useful, their level of motivation increases exponentially. If your students make English-speaking friends or take summer jobs working with English-speaking supervisors, co-workers, and clients, expect a surge of interest. If a student becomes romantically involved with a native speaker of English, expect interest to skyrocket. Reaching a plateau, any plateau, also makes a great difference. After a reluctant student understands a movie or a popular song, expect a positive attitude adjustment. You may find that, after dragging their feet for a year or two, some students suddenly decide that they are ready to buckle down. You will then, of course, welcome the prodigal students into the fold of serious learners. When you see a new level of motivation, take advantage of it.

Working With Younger Students

Younger students tend to master languages more quickly than do older ones. This is in part because they do not have as far to go. A four-year-old with a vocabulary of a few thousand words would be considered a near-native speaker. A twelve-year-old with the same vocabulary would be considered a beginner.

There are other factors as well. Linguist Noam Chomsky hypothesizes that the minds of small children possess a language acquisition device, or LAD, that enables them to absorb language easily. Not all linguists and psychologists agree that the LAD exists. It is certain, however, that those who are thoroughly immersed in a language as small children can eventually learn to speak it without syntactical errors or an accent. This rarely occurs with those who begin to learn a language during or after adolescence.

Language Learning and Early Literacy

When considering how long young children should stay in an ESL or bilingual program, it is important to consider their double academic burden. Those who begin school not speaking English must learn their new language and basic literacy skills concurrently. If they are taught reading in their native language, there will be less time to learn English. If they learn to read in English, initial reading progress will likely be slower than that of students who learn to read in their native language. Young children will not outread their oral vocabularies. A young student is likely to learn enough English to communicate more quickly than an older one, but that progress may have come at the expense of early literacy skills. A program that stresses early oral English above literacy is not necessarily bad, as long as the literacy issue is adequately addressed at an appropriate time.

5

Using the Learner's Native Language in the Classroom

Whether or not academic subjects should be taught in the students' native language as they are in the bilingual education classroom is indeed a controversial topic, one that will not be addressed here. There are advantages to teaching students to read in the language they speak, and there are advantages to studying academic subjects in the language the students understand best, but there are also advantages to providing English learners with as much contact with English as possible. Suffice it to say that this question is beyond the scope of this book. This section will instead deal with the use of the learner's native language in the ESL classroom, the mainstream, and the ESL component of the bilingual class schedule.

Most students will not be able to communicate in English beyond a survival level until they have had several hundred hours of English language contact, instruction, and interaction. Even the very quickest learners will require literally thousands of hours before they attain near-native fluency. Clearly "the phrase of the day" or a daily half-hour of English conversation will not bring students to fluency in a few years. Although using the students' native language will not hinder the learning of English, time spent communicating in the native language is time not spent communicating in

English. Your students will not get sufficient contact with English if they spend most of their ESL class time merely talking about English in their native language.

There are, of course, a few no-brainer situations. When you explain how to get out of the building in case of a fire or how to operate the eye bath in the chemistry lab, you need to be absolutely certain that everyone understands. In such situation, to not use the students' native language or allow a student or staff member to translate into the native language could be considered even criminally negligent.

If you choose to use the students' native language in your lessons, be certain that it enhances rather than detracts from English instruction. It is important to *not* consistently provide side-by-side translations for everything you say in English. There are two reasons for this. First, the human mind, like flowing water, seeks the course of least resistance. If your students are expecting that everything important is going to be repeated in their native language, their brains will automatically shut down when they hear English. If you are going to use the native language in your ESL class, do not use it consistently or predictably. Keep your students on their toes when you speak English.

Also bear in mind that it is easier for someone who is struggling with a new language to follow speech in that language when the speaker is not always switching back and forth. The graduate-level Spanish literature class in which I learned the least was taught by a professor who kept stopping her lectures to make English-language explanations to the three non-Hispanic students in the class. The frequent switching into English made it harder to follow what she was saying in Spanish. People who are fully fluent in two languages have little trouble switching, but it is tougher for those who are still learning. Our professor was not, as she believed, doing us a favor.

DON'T FORCE THEM TO GO MUTE

Although it is essential that students have sufficient contact with English, a total prohibition on the use of the students' native language in school will likely prove unwise. Students who cannot speak English but are not allowed to speak anything else may respond by going mute, sometimes for years. This is not an exaggeration. If you choose to speak to your students only in English, during the first few months of the course it would be wise to allow them to respond in their native language either to you or to a bilingual assistant, at least at specified times. It would also be wise to provide after-class sessions when someone could answer students' questions in their native language. That is far better than having them spend the entire year sitting in silence.

WHAT WORKS BEST IN THE STUDENTS' NATIVE LANGUAGE

Some English lessons are best taught partially in the learners' native language. If a teacher is explaining how a certain grammatical structure parallels that of the students' native language, a brief explanation in the native language may help the student to immediately grasp a concept that might otherwise take months to figure out. Postlesson explanations and advance organizers are also appropriate. If a student does not understand a lecture, it is acceptable to give an explanation in the native language after class or outside of class. It may also be useful to provide an explanation or synopsis as an advance organizer in the native language before watching a movie or reading a work of literature. Such an explanation will help your students follow the thread of the work. Use your own judgment in these matters. Some of the less motivated students may use native-language sessions as a way to glean enough material to limp through your tests and as an excuse to pay less attention to what is said in English. If you see this happening, scale back on the amount of native language used in class.

Although there are dangers in the use of frequent side-by-side translations, in some instances they can be useful. When a student needs to know the meaning of a word or a phrase that cannot be demonstrated or explained in English, and a translation is the quickest or most efficient way to convey the meaning, by all means translate, but do so quickly and move immediately back into English.

CONSIDER THE LANGUAGE AND THE CULTURE OF THE COMMUNITY

When choosing whether or not to allow the use of the native language, consider the nature of the linguistic community. In a border community or an ethnic enclave where most people are bilingual, it may be unwise to be the only person in school who will not tolerate the use of the students' native language.

On the Texas-Mexico border where I teach, the parents of some of my students have unpleasant memories of being punished for speaking Spanish in school. If you impose an English-only rule, be sure that your students and their parents understand that this rule is to enhance the learning of English and is not in any way meant to disparage their language and culture. By the way, it will be easier to convince them of your good intentions if you happen to be able to speak their language reasonably well.

USE TIME LIMITS

If you use the students' native language in the ESL classroom, it will be tempting to use it excessively. Again, the mind seeks the course of least resistance, and that means finding the best common language. It is easier and more pleasant to speak when people understand you. One way to avoid this tendency is to set aside certain times for use of the native language. If you are teaching a three-hour ESL block, you could set aside one half-hour per day or a short period at the beginning or end of each class during which use of the native language is permitted but not used exclusively. During that time you can entertain questions, discuss school rules and procedures, translate vocabulary, make grammatical explanations, or provide advance organizers or postlesson explanations.

Working With Younger Students

The balance between native language and English use in ESL instruction should be much the same for both younger and older students. If, however, you work in a bilingual program in which content classes are taught almost exclusively in the native language and only an hour or two per day is allocated specifically for English instruction, finding time for sufficient contact with English can be a problem. In such a situation, use English as much as possible in nonacademic situations.

6

Natural and Unnatural Approaches to Learning English

Sixteenth-century grammarian Desiderius Erasmus and Latin teacher Bishop J. A. Comenius disagreed about the roles of conversation and grammar in the teaching of Latin. Comenius argued against the use of grammar study, whereas Erasmus proposed teaching Latin through a combination of conversation and grammar.

Comenius's style of language teaching was reborn in the nineteenth century as the natural approach, an approach to language teaching that relies heavily on oral language. Nineteenth-century Europe also gave rise to the direct method, which probably would have had Erasmus's approval. The direct method is a hybrid of grammar and natural methodology that employs conversation but pays heed to structure.

Since Erasmus's time, and probably for centuries before that, the language teaching pendulum has swung back and forth between the extremes of analytical methods that involve the study of grammar and experiential methods that are based on oral language use.

THE NATURAL APPROACH: LEARNING ENGLISH BY HEARING AND SPEAKING IT

The natural approach was popularized more recently (relative to Comenius's era at least) by University of Southern California education professor Steven Krashen and his associate Tracy Terrell. The modern version of the natural approach emphasizes presenting the language naturally in pieces that the student can understand without resorting to translation. Krashen calls these intelligible bits of target language *comprehensible input*.

Krashen recommends creating a pleasant classroom environment and communicating in a manner that is 90% intelligible to the students. The teacher can do this by demonstrating while speaking or by using familiar vocabulary and context clues. Krashen differentiates between language learning, which occurs as the result of formal study, and acquisition, which is the result of contact and practice. Krashen insists that the latter is more effective. He also theorizes that there is a silent period during which a learner hears and learns but is not yet prepared to produce.

Perhaps the best known of Krashen's theories is the *monitor theory*. According to this theory, the mind absorbs language, but an affective filter may get in the way of this natural process. When the teacher creates a pleasant environment along with comprehensible input, the affective filter is lowered and language acquisition occurs. He theorizes that there is another mental device called the *monitor* that can edit thoughts and utterances and allow a speaker to consciously control speech, but that this process is part of learning and not the more efficient acquisition.

It is hard to argue with the notion that one should learn by doing. In the case of language learning (or acquisition, as Krashen would say), this means learning to understand a language by hearing it and to speak a language by speaking it. A strong argument for the natural approach is the fact that almost all human beings manage to learn their primary language simply by being immersed in it.

Inert and Active Knowledge

It is possible to understand bits of knowledge but not be able to apply them. An English learner might know that a certain letter makes a certain sound but he may not be able to produce that sound or even differentiate it from similar sounds. He might know the meaning of a certain word but not be able to say or even recognize that word when he hears it, or he might be able to recognize the word in isolation but not be able to pick it out of a sentence. He might know that *ed* attached to a verb indicates the past tense, yet he might not be able to apply that rule quickly and automatically enough to use it in conversation, either to produce an oral sentence in the past tense or to understand the tense of a sentence he hears.

Knowledge that one has but cannot readily apply is sometimes called *inert knowledge*, while that which one can apply is called *active knowledge*. It is easier to impart inert knowledge, but active knowledge is clearly more useful. There are people who have learned pages of German vocabulary and the conjugations of hundreds of German verbs yet would still have trouble ordering a bratwurst and a beer in Berlin.

Active and Inert Knowledge of the Metric System

Consider how you learned the metric system. If you know the formulae for converting between ounces and pounds and grams and kilos but do not know how many grams or kilos different items weigh without doing a conversion, your knowledge of the metric system is inert. If you know that you weigh 75 kilos, that your car weighs 1,000 kilos, that your neighbor's SUV weighs 2,000 kilos, that a 300-gram steak is enough for a hearty meal, and that 50 grams of cheese is enough for a nice sandwich, you possess active knowledge of metric weights. Although it is easier to learn to divide pounds by 2.2 or to multiply ounces times 28 than it is to weigh thousands of items on a metric scale, it is easier to work with metric weights after you have weighed a certain number of items on a metric scale and noted their metric weights. In like manner, direct use of the language enables and enhances active knowledge of it.

Some Problems With the Natural Approach

That having been said, a few problems exist with the modern version of the natural approach. The premise that students can learn a second language the same way that they learned their first is flawed. Although young children seem to absorb second languages as naturally and effortlessly as they do their first, this does not appear to occur with adolescents and adults. Americans traveling abroad find surprisingly few American residents, even long-term residents, who speak the local language well. It is not uncommon to find Americans abroad who, even after 20 years living immersed in the local language, must rely on interpreters for all but the most basic communication. There are also a great many immigrants in the United States whose command of English is still poor, even after decades of English language contact.

Even if it were possible to absorb a second language the same way we acquired the first, the classroom is an artificial environment and cannot perfectly replicate a first-language learning experience. We begin to learn our first language through years of one-on-one interaction with our caregivers. If the classes are large, the teacher cannot have more than a few minutes per day of one-on-one interaction with each student. In addition, the sort of vocabulary and structures that students other than small children will need in school are not so easily absorbed. It is easy to make

"I am jumping" comprehensible. Expressions like, "I wouldn't have done that if I had known you didn't want me to" are a different matter.

APPLYING FIRST LANGUAGE
SKILLS TO SECOND LANGUAGE LEARNING

Those who firmly believe in building knowledge of a second language entirely from the ground up are reminiscent of the protagonist in Jorge Borges's short story, "Pierre Menard, Author of *Don Quijote*." In this tale the protagonist decides to replicate for himself all of the experiences of Miguel de Cervantes in the hope that he will be able to write (not copy) the entire text of the great novel *Don Quijote* exactly as Cervantes had written it. English learners bring knowledge and skills that can carry over from their native language to English. Those who argue for the exclusive use of natural approaches ignore the value of this carryover.

BALANCING EXPERIENTIAL
AND ANALYTICAL APPROACHES

As Erasmus discovered centuries ago, an intelligent balance between experiential and analytical study of a language will bear fruit. Authentic use of the language teaches students to respond easily and automatically to the language as they hear it. The study of grammar allows learners to apply what they know of their native language to the target language and to discover syntactic and morphological patterns that they might never absorb without formal study. The rote study of vocabulary allows them to learn vocabulary, especially abstract vocabulary, more quickly than they could by just using the language.

Teachers who use natural techniques are able to present less material in a given period of time than those who work with word lists and drills, but authentic language use is more likely to instill active knowledge of the language. A foreign language teacher who has students for a mere 45 minutes per day for just a year or two must choose between imparting a lot of inert knowledge or less but more useful active knowledge of the language. ESL teachers who are allotted sufficient time to teach their subject well do not have to face this dilemma.

Getting Started, Naturally

The natural approach can be used effectively in the classroom as long as the teacher understands its limitations. It is essential to understand which concepts are best taught through the natural approach and under which conditions. Natural methods can be especially effective early in a beginning ESL course, and it is wise to use them extensively at least during the first two months or so. At that point most of the vocabulary should be concrete and, even though the teacher will speak using various tenses and structures, the students should not be expected to understand them all. In the first few months of study, most students will pick words out of English sentences and respond to them, as they will likely not understand all that is said.

It is not necessary to enforce the silent period at this time, but it is best to honor it. At this early point, students should not yet be required to speak or write, although they may attempt to do so if they wish. Class size makes a big difference with this approach. The larger the class, the less interaction will be possible between teacher and student, so the less effective the natural approach will be, unless English-speaking volunteers are available.

USING TOTAL PHYSICAL RESPONSE (TPR)

Some seminatural techniques, however, can be used in large classrooms. One of the most effective for large groups of beginners is Total Physical Response (TPR), a technique developed by San Jose State University psychology professor James Asher. In this technique, the teacher demonstrates an action or indicates an object, describes it, and then gives a command to the students. You might point and say, "I am pointing," and then command, "Point!" If the students do not understand, repeat, "Point!" and move a student's hand into a pointing gesture. Then point to a door, a window, and a desk, describing each object as you do so, and ask students to point at those objects.

You can even move into more difficult concepts with TPR. Ask students to point to the ball that is not red, or to give the ball to someone else. At this point the students should not be asked to repeat these commands, but rather merely to respond to them. When you ask them to produce these structures either in oral or written form a few weeks or months later, their task will be easier because of the foundation laid through TPR. If you have a three-hour block to teach ESL, you can easily cover a 1,000-word vocabulary in two months using this technique. Appendix 1, the vocabulary lists at the end of this book, lists several common concrete words and expressions that lend themselves well to TPR and other oral-language-based techniques.

LANGUAGE IN THE FOREGROUND AND THE BACKGROUND

Brain studies give us some interesting insights into language learning. Electroencephalograms done on people who are speaking a language with which they are not familiar indicate wave activity all over the brain, while those who are speaking a language that they know well have wave activity concentrated in a much smaller area. When we formally study a language, we learn with great conscious effort. Let us call this "constructing language in the foreground of the mind." Students at this point have to concentrate so much on the language itself that it is difficult for them to actually use the language as a tool to understand and communicate. When people speak with reasonable fluency, there is less conscious effort and words flow effortlessly. When this occurs, language is what it should be, a tool of communication. Let us call this phenomenon "constructing language in the background."

Clearly it is desirable to lead students to this point as quickly as possible. This does not mean that language should never be studied in the foreground. That which is learned in the foreground can be practiced in the background. Because we usually use our native language without paying conscious attention to the language itself, it is good to practice second languages in the same way. When possible, review old structures and vocabulary in the background at the same time that you present new material. Once students have at least a tenuous grasp on the past tense, steer them toward its use when you present or practice other tenses, new vocabulary, or different kinds of sentences. When you speak with your students, use structures and vocabulary with which they are already familiar. When they speak to you, try to steer them into practicing what they have learned. Conversation makes the best review.

Academic study in English will naturally enhance language learning once students reach an intermediate level, but even with beginners you may do activities in which other academic skills are brought into the foreground in order to force language into the background. Simple arithmetic is a good way to take students' conscious minds off the learning of numbers. When you ask students to add, subtract, multiply, or divide mentally, and you allow them too little time to translate mentally, the computation occupies their conscious minds, forcing the learning of numbers into the subconscious. For older students, simple algebra is a good way to drill letters as well. *If x plus 7 equals 9, what is the value of x? If b minus 10 equals 15, what is the value of b? If 9f equals 72, what is the value of f?* While teaching in Japan, I found that most Japanese students in the fourth grade could handle such equations. That should give some of our math teachers a bit of a scare.

WINNING OVER THE SKEPTICS IN YOUR SCHOOL

Some educators have strong opinions about natural approaches, either for or against. If your administrators or peers are in the "against" camp, they may observe you and conclude that you are wasting time. There are those who feel that learning is taking place only when there is tangible proof, like a completed worksheet, to show at the end of class. Administrators, fellow teachers, parents, or students who do not understand the language-learning process may accuse competent language teachers of being too easy on students early in the year when they are teaching mostly oral language, and then accuse the same teachers of being too tough later in the course after they begin to pile on written work. It is not that these teachers get more demanding as the year progresses, but rather that the nature of the lessons changes as the students move ahead. To everything there is a season. If anyone objects to intensive use of oral language, show the nonbelievers the vocabulary you are teaching and the structures you are presenting. They will probably be astounded at the large amount of vocabulary you pack into your "play" lessons. If possible, give detractors a short, private lesson in a language they do not understand. That should make it clear to them that these natural lessons are not mere play.

Working With Younger Students

Natural and seminatural techniques are appropriate for all ages and levels, but teachers of young students will want to use them more than will teachers of older students. Teachers in early elementary school may want to use TPR throughout the first year of language instruction because most of what small children can understand even in their native language can be touched or demonstrated.

Natural techniques encourage the student to respond to English without going through the native language. Once students are able to respond directly to English, they can more efficiently get language from all sources available to them. Because older students have reading and writing skills, they will be able to get much of their language from print media. Younger students depend more heavily on the spoken word.

7

Building Vocabulary

They'll Need Lots

The English lexicon tips the scales at more than 600,000 words. Of course, no single speaker of English knows all of them, but an extremely intelligent, well-educated native speaker might know as many as 250,000. Even a typical native speaker in middle school should know more than 25,000. If you are a college-educated native speaker of English, chances are that there are few words in a dictionary of 100,000 entries that you do not understand. As if the sheer numbers are not intimidating enough, students must learn to hear, say, read, and write each word. And then there are those pesky nuances, homonyms, multiple meanings, idioms, and so forth.

The good news is that a language learner with a much smaller vocabulary can still communicate effectively. Speakers will use high-frequency words hundreds of times per day but will use some low-frequency words only a few times in a lifetime. Knowledge of 1,000 words plus a basic grasp of structure allows a learner to function in English. A student at this level may be said to speak survival-level English. At this point one can get around and get by without the aid of an interpreter. Between 1,000 and 2,000 words actually make up a full 80% of everything that most people say. In the case of younger people like your students, the low figure is the more accurate. Of course, many of those thousand are function words, and a missing 20% makes a big hole on a page.

A 5,000-word vocabulary along with a fair grasp of structure is sufficient to communicate intelligently on nontechnical subjects. Call this level oral BICS (basic interpersonal communication skills) if you like. High school students at this level who have reasonably good academic skills in their native language should be able to function in the mainstream at least part of the day if they are willing to use bilingual dictionaries frequently. A mere 15 words per day will allow students of English to reach this functional level in one year. If they spend eight hours per day with English, that works out to less than one new word per half hour. Bear in mind, however, that many school-aged native English speakers add an average of 15 new words to their vocabularies daily, so English learners who hope to catch up with their native-English-speaking classmates should aspire to learn considerably more.

If you teach an ESL block that consumes at least half the school day, it is reasonable to present and test students on approximately 100 words per week. Also, English learners should be encouraged to attempt to learn another 100 per week on their own. At that pace, even with a mere 60% mastery, students will acquire sufficient vocabulary for survival-level English in about two months, BICS in a year, and the means to successfully compete with native speakers in three years. Very few students are not capable of learning to at least understand 100 words per week if they are given adequate exposure and practice, although some students might require some prodding before they do so.

ENJOYING THE PATH TO A LARGE VOCABULARY

Vocabulary learning need not be painful. Much can be painlessly absorbed through the natural techniques described in Chapter 6. More can be absorbed watching television, listening to songs, or talking with friends. This does not mean that endless hours spent watching MTV can take the place of studying, but all contact with English has value. Once students hit the 2,000-word threshold, they will be able to deduce much meaning from context. A student with such a vocabulary who hears "The lion was chasing an impala across the veldt" should be able to deduce that an impala is an African animal and the veldt is a sort of land found in Africa.

All of us assimilate vocabulary in this way in our native language, although as adults we do not encounter much new vocabulary in our everyday language use. Those who are immersed in second languages encounter hundreds of new words each day, and the meaning of a great many of them can be deduced through context.

Those who have learned foreign languages understand this process well. Monolingual readers can get a sense of this process by reading Anthony Burgess's novel, *A Clockwork Orange*. Alex, the narrator and anti-hero, is a futuristic juvenile delinquent who speaks Nadsat, an odd slang, much of which is borrowed from Russian. The slang is presented in such a way that the reader can usually deduce the meaning from context. Where the context is not clear, Burgess has his narrator use appositives. Alex and his droogs, Pete, Georgie, and Dim, other malchicks about his age, drink moloko at the Korova Milkbar. The four droogs meet at the milkbar to peet moloko and viddy other malchicks and pretty devotchkas and spend their deng. They viddy people who come out of the nearby biblio with books that they had checked out or watch them read the news in the gazetta. When a droog makes a comment that Alex does not like, Alex tells him to shut his bloody rot.

It becomes clear that *malchick* means boy, *droog* means friend, p*eet* means drink, *biblio* means library, *deng* means money, *gazetta* means newspaper, *rot* means mouth, and so on. After reading *A Clockwork Orange*, an attentive reader will understand scores of Russian words. Try it yourself. After only a few hours of reading, you will find that Russian-like words have invaded your thoughts. Bear in mind that these words have been presented in the Roman alphabet and that the reader understands them only when they are pronounced using English sounds. Also, verb inflections and other grammatical features are 100%English. Nevertheless, the experience of carefully reading *A Clockwork Orange* should give you an idea of how quickly vocabulary can be absorbed in context.

LEARNING FROM THE MOVIES

For students who are competent readers of either English or their native language, subtitled movies offer a fun and relatively painless way to build vocabulary. Viewers can either read the subtitles in English as they listen in their native language, or vice versa. In this manner, they might pick up 20 or 30 new words from a single movie without even being aware of having done so. Be warned, however, that this technique does not always work perfectly. Text is not always translated accurately, for a number of reasons. A student once entered my classroom and announced, "This room sucks." Because he was not a troublesome sort, I assumed that his comment was the result of a misunderstanding. When I asked him what he meant, he told me in Spanish, *Esta sala apesta*, which means "This room stinks." The room had recently been cleaned with a foul-smelling detergent and did indeed stink. The previous night he had watched a subtitled movie in which a partygoer declared, "This party sucks!" while the subtitle read, *Esta fiesta apesta* (This party stinks).

Many DVDs have subtitles in several languages and multiple sound tracks. If your students are Spanish or French speakers, it will be easy to find DVDs that they can play in both English and their native language. Such DVDs are available in other languages as well, but they will be more difficult to find. Learners can watch the film in their native language while they read subtitles in English and then listen in English while they read in their native language. Or they can watch mostly in English, replaying scenes with subtitles only when they find them necessary. Bear in mind that this technique works with motivated learners only. Less interested students might spend hours mindlessly caught up in car chases, shootouts, and special effects without benefiting much linguistically.

TEACHING VOCABULARY WITH PICTURE DICTIONARIES

Picture dictionaries with themed pages are great tools for presenting concrete vocabulary. These dictionaries may be used to look up words or they may be used to present vocabulary thematically. Students may study a page about a kitchen the same week that they read a story or a textbook chapter with a lot of kitchen vocabulary. Or you may present a Total Physical Response (TPR) lesson in a real kitchen. The picture dictionary allows students to review TPR vocabulary or vocabulary taken from a written lesson at home without having to translate.

My personal favorite is the American English version of the *Oxford Picture Dictionary*. This dictionary covers a vocabulary of nearly 4,000 words grouped into 140 categories. It is available in a generic version that gives the words in English only, or in bilingual versions that offer translations into different languages. This dictionary also has accompanying tapes so that learners who are not yet competent English readers can hear the words as they look at the pictures. It also includes an interactive CD ROM.

USING VOCABULARY FROM THE NATIVE LANGUAGE

Most of your students will come to your class knowing a great many words that resemble English words. This is especially true of those who speak Indo-European languages, but as the world has shrunk Anglicisms have found their ways into all of the world's major languages. Chances are your students will not understand the English cognates (words in different languages that resemble one another in both sound and meaning) for words in their native tongues at first, but as they master the English phonological system the cognates will become easier to hear and identify. When this happens, they will find that they have stumbled upon a bonus of hundreds or even thousands of free words. Using these cognates can greatly facilitate that first difficult step into English.

A few words of warning, however: Some cognates are a far stretch. The *oke* in the Japanese *karaoke*, rendered *kareoke* in English, is actually the

Japanese cognate for the English word *orchestra*, and *suto* is a cognate for *strike*, abbreviated from *sutoraiko*. And some cognates are false. The Spanish word *embarazada* means *pregnant*, not *embarrassed*, and *condesendente* means *sycophantic*, or *boot-licking*, not *condescending*. More often that not, however, the cognates will have a more-or-less equivalent meaning in the two languages. Early in the process of language learning, it is best for your students to assume that the cognates are equivalent until proven otherwise.

BUILDING VOCABULARY WITH WORD BLOCKS

Although students will need to learn tens of thousands of words before they attain native-like fluency, many of those words are variations of a single root word. If students know the affixes *un, ness*, and *ly*, upon learning *happy* they will also automatically understand the words *happiness, happily, unhappy, unhappily*, and *unhappiness*. Key prefixes and suffixes can be found in good dictionaries, grammar books, or ESL textbooks.

IDIOMS AND OTHER CONFUSING EXPRESSIONS

There is a great Tex Avery cartoon that features a speaker who uses idioms and slang expressions, while a listener tries to interpret what he hears. When the speaker says, "I was short handed," the listener imagines the speaker with tiny arms. Upon hearing, "We painted the town red and really put on the dog," he imagines a man painting a storefront while his girlfriend wears a collie like a stole. When he hears about caring for little ones, he imagines someone tending small numerals.

Idioms can be confusing for language learners. One must learn hundreds in the process of learning a language. Pick a good dictionary and look up the word "get." You will find between a quarter and a half page of idioms: *get up, get out, get over, get away with, get after*, and so on. These expressions cannot be translated literally, and one who tries to do so will end up like the listener in the cartoon. When teaching idioms, it is best to teach students to think of an idiom as a single concept, not the sum of the words that comprise it. Most textbooks include idioms along with their vocabulary words. Good dictionaries include idioms along with word definitions.

LOOK IT UP! LEARNING ENGLISH WITH DICTIONARIES

Movies, pictures, and songs are useful and fun, but do not write off dictionary use. Context does not always make new vocabulary clear. While

Burgess wrote *A Clockwork Orange* in a manner that makes Alex's Russian-like slang easily intelligible, works of literature do not always provide context clues that clarify new vocabulary. Concrete vocabulary is best taught with objects, pictures, and actions, at least to beginners, but not all vocabulary is concrete. It is easy to demonstrate opening a window or zipping up a jacket, but it is not so easy to demonstrate the social, political, and economic upheavals that led to the French Revolution. More sophisticated vocabulary is not so easily represented with drawings and pictures. It is easy to draw a tree that all of your students recognize as a tree, but how about an oak or an ash?

When your students get past vocabulary that can be easily demonstrated, it will be time to hand out dictionaries. For beginning and intermediate students who are literate in their native languages, a bilingual dictionary is a must after the first semester. For English learners who lack a strong native language dominance or those who never learned to read well in their native language, a regular English dictionary may prove more useful than a bilingual one. Children's dictionaries are good for beginning English learners, even the older ones, because the definitions are written in simple language.

You will find that your students most easily learn vocabulary related to subjects that interest them. A sports fan may learn words like *goaltender*, *fullback*, and *stadium* with little effort, and an amateur photographer might learn words like *lens*, *shutter*, *aperture*, and *f-stop* even before learning survival vocabulary. If you are tutoring one on one, you have the luxury of tailoring your lessons to your student's interest. Most of us are not so lucky. Students in larger classes can, however, direct their own vocabulary learning using their own dictionaries.

Encourage students to look up words related to their favorite subjects and write them down. When you have a spare moment, engage your students in conversations that employ those words, or encourage them to use those words when they speak English with friends, classmates, and volunteer tutors. Encourage your students to mentally compose three or four sentences with each of the words they look up. When students look up words in text they are reading, have them write the words down or lightly mark them in the book with pencil and then compose the mental sentences later.

Many bilingual dictionaries use the International Phonetic Alphabet (IPA) to show how words are pronounced, although a few use the long/short vowel system, and a few make up their own system. Because the IPA is the most commonly used system in bilingual dictionaries, it will prove to be the most useful. There will be further discussion of the IPA in Chapter 10.

A number of excellent bilingual dictionaries are on the market. In selecting one, keep in mind the native-language reading level of your students. Many brands of dictionaries are available in one language only, although some publishers produce dictionaries in different languages. Larousse publishes excellent bilingual dictionaries in several languages, but their level may be too high for elementary or middle school students or for high school students or adults who are poor readers in their native language. If you teach older students, you might ask them which dictionaries work best for them, or keep several kinds of dictionaries in your classroom and see which ones your students gravitate to. If you can read your students' native language, you can help decide which dictionary is best for them. If not, you could ask bilingual people on your school staff or in your community for recommendations.

ELECTRONIC DICTIONARIES

If you have computers in your classroom, dictionary software will prove to be quite useful. Several good bilingual dictionaries exist for personal computers and PDAs on the market. Good, reasonably priced hand-held electronic bilingual dictionaries are available as well. The advantage of the electronic dictionaries is that they are fast. For a student who needs to consult a dictionary 20 times per page, that extra speed makes a big difference. Talking dictionaries, which pronounce the word, are especially useful for beginning students or students who are poor readers.

Some of these programs, like the software version of the *Merriam-Webster Dictionary* or the *American Heritage Talking Dictionary*, can be linked directly to a word processor, and some bilingual word processors have bilingual dictionaries built into them. Students can copy and paste text into the word-processor program and have automatic access to the dictionary as they read. If you have a dictionary program that does not link automatically, you or a reasonably knowledgeable computer user can create a macro that will create a link. You can also find programs that offer text with hotwords that link to definitions. Some reference programs like *Microsoft Encarta* or *Compton's Interactive Encyclopedia* have their entire text linked to a dictionary, so readers can click any word and get a definition immediately.

Bilingual dictionaries for PDAs provide translations for words with the tap of a stylus. English learners can download ebooks on PDAs that they can carry in their shirt pockets and read at their leisure. Appendix 2 includes the names of Web sites where public domain literature can be downloaded free of charge.

THOSE BORING VOCABULARY LISTS

Vocabulary lists may not be particularly popular, but they serve an important purpose. However, students should not be expected to know a word simply because they have seen it on a list. Learners should hear, say, read, and write each word several times in a variety of contexts. Use the words in context in class several times, present them with pictures if possible, and create situations that oblige the students to both say and write them. Have students periodically do a self-check in which they read over the week's vocabulary and note and study those words they do not understand. While you should not expect students to learn vocabulary just from a list, let the list support vocabulary learning.

LAYERED VOCABULARY LEARNING

It is important to remember that we do not learn all of the aspects, definitions, and nuances of a word at once. From the sentence, "There was a lovely gardenia in the bouquet that Johnny gave to his mother," one can conclude that a gardenia is a flower. When learners see a picture of a gardenia, their knowledge of that flower increases. If they see, touch, and smell a real gardenia, that knowledge increases again. If they study the life cycle of the gardenia in biology class, they will know even more.

Students might learn the meaning of the word *accolade* from a television sports announcer who was referring to an honor that had been conferred on an athlete. They might later see the word in print, sound it out, and add it to their reading vocabulary. Later still they might learn from a dictionary or deduce from a book of medieval history or a novel about King Arthur that *accolade* also means a tap on a knight's shoulder with a sword. When practice has embedded words solidly in students' minds, it is a simple matter to add more meaning to those words at a later time.

Working With Younger Students

The older the student, the more useful bilingual dictionary use will be. Picture dictionaries will be useful for all ages. The *Oxford Picture Dictionary* is appropriate for upper elementary school and beyond. Several illustrated picture dictionaries are on the market for younger children. Films are useful for all ages, although the subtitles do not work well for the younger ones.

Small children seem to be better at "absorbing" new vocabulary through mere exposure than are older learners. With very young children, modeling vocabulary matters more than drilling it.

8

Grammar

The Skeletal System of the Language

ME VERY GRAMMAR

Once, when I was teaching intermediate ESL to adults, the teacher of the advanced class sent me one of her students. He had requested placement in the advanced group because he had studied English in his native country, but the material proved too difficult for him. The same proved true in my intermediate class. After an hour of struggle he shouted, "Me very grammar. You class no grammar!" and stormed out of the room.

Many people claim that they know the grammar of a language yet cannot compose intelligible sentences when they attempt to speak it. Grammar exercises taught in isolation can kill a lot of time and still leave the learner unable to produce a grammatical sentence. As part of a balanced course, however, the study of grammar can greatly enhance understanding and fluency. Grammar is simply a study of the rules that govern a language. Those rules are the skeleton upon which we hang the vocabulary. They can be mastered consciously, and through practice their application can become as automatic as they are for native speakers. My former student's grammar lessons had taken him only half way. He understood the rules but was not able to apply them.

Do not assume that students will automatically absorb the rules of grammar. Sometimes it works out that way, especially with young students, but not always. A number of English learners manage to assimilate thousands of words of English vocabulary over several years yet have only the most tenuous grasp of English structure. Such individuals can express themselves with isolated or poorly connected words yet are quite limited in overall communication. If you are fortunate enough to have such students in your class, you may have the chance to dazzle your superiors and amaze your peers. Some vocabulary-rich but structure-poor students can be led from the "me-Tarzan-you-Jane" level to reasonable fluency in a few months.

WHEN TO START GRAMMAR LESSONS

It is best to avoid teaching explicit grammar until students have at least a survival command of the language. When they understand and can respond to a thousand words or so and have begun to at least attempt to produce sentences, they are probably ready. By this time, they should have already heard thousands of grammatical English sentences, and their mental fields should be well tilled by contact with their new language.

ENGLISH GRAMMAR ISN'T AS TOUGH AS WE THINK

As grammars go, that of English is not so complicated, even though we English-speaking chauvinists like to imagine that we have one of the most difficult languages in the world. Most of our verbs have only four forms, and only one, *to be,* has more than five. Only about fifty verbs of consequence are irregular, and most of them are irregular only in the past tense. No verb suffixes reflect politeness or respect, as with many Asian languages. English does not have masculine and feminine articles, and only our pronouns have cases.

FREEBIES: WHEN ENGLISH GRAMMAR MATCHES THE LEARNER'S NATIVE LANGUAGE

When an English structure parallels that of the learner's native language, a simple grammatical explanation can lead to immediate mastery. If a Spanish speaker knows grammatical terminology in his or her own language and knows how to form the past participle of common English verbs, it is a small matter to teach the perfect mood, because the perfect in Spanish exactly mirrors that of English. Because *he* and *han* mean *have,* and the suffix *ado* is the equivalent to the English *ed*, it is easy for such a student to understand that *Yo he estudiado* is the same as "I have studied" or that *Ellos han brincado* means "They have jumped." Structures that do not parallel those in the students' native language will be more difficult, but not impossible, to learn.

THE GARDEN PATH TO ENGLISH GRAMMAR

A complete grammar lesson is, of course, beyond the scope of this book, but here is the quick-start version. Mastery of verbs and a knowledge of word order are sufficient to permit students to compose intelligible sentences in English. It is acceptable to tell your beginning students that mastery of the verb entails most of English grammar. By the time the students figure out that you were exaggerating, they will be advanced enough to have experienced success with their new language and will thus not turn back. Here is the garden path, or the easy way, to mastery of the English verb.

Regular English verbs have only three inflections: the third person singular *s* or its variant *es*, *ed* to form the past tense and the past participle, and *ing* to form the present participle and the gerund.

There are four classes of auxiliary verbs. The forms of *to be* (*is, am, are, was, were*) combine with the present participle to form the progressive tenses (*I am singing, they were singing*) and with the past participle to form the passive voice (*Italian was spoken, English is spoken, French will be spoken*). The modals *can, could, should, would, might, must, may, will,* and *shall* combine with other verbs without any inflections (*I can work, you will play*). The perfect is formed with *have, has, had,* followed by the past participle (*they have studied, it had rained*). The past participle is usually the same as the past tense, although there are about 20 common exceptions.

When an auxiliary verb is present, or the verb is a form of *to be*, form the negative by adding the word *not* or the contraction *n't. He is happy; he is not (or isn't) sad. We should study; we should not (or shouldn't) waste time.* Otherwise, make the sentence negative by adding "do not," "does not," "did not," or their contractions "don't," "doesn't," or "didn't" before the main verb. *I don't like broccoli; he didn't arrive late.*

When an auxiliary verb is present, form the question by reversing the subject and the auxiliary verb. *Mary is swimming* becomes *Is Mary swimming? John can help us* becomes *Can John help us?* If the verb is the copula, reverse the subject and the verb. *We are late* becomes *Are we late?*

The simple present is the most difficult tense to teach. It has two forms, and the interrogative and the negative are formed with an auxiliary *do* or its third person variant *does.* Also complicating matters is that there are three ways to pronounce the third person inflectional *s.* Except for the third person singular, the simple present is only the simple form of the verb. The third person singular adds *s* or *es,* depending on the final phoneme. The inflexion *es* follows *s* and the *s*-like sounds, soft *c,* soft *g, sh, ch, z,* and *x.* After these sounds the *e* of *es* is never silent. Following a voiced sound (any vowel, *b, d, g, l, m, n, r, v,* or *w*) the inflectional *s* is pronounced like a *z.* In other cases, it is the sibilant *s.*

To form the negative, we place the auxiliary *do not/don't* or *does not/doesn't* between the subject and the main verb. The latter is for negative statements in the third person singular. The former is for all others. The question is formed by placing *do/does* before the subject, while the main verb follows the subject. Following the auxiliary *does* in either the question or the negative statement, the inflectional *s* is not added to the main verb.

The simple past of the affirmative statement is formed in most cases by simply adding the suffix *ed*. As with the inflectional *s*, the *ed* is pronounced three different ways, depending on the preceding sound. After *d* and *t*, the *e* of *ed* is pronounced. In other cases, it is silent. After voiced sounds (all vowels, *b, g, j, l, m, n, r, v, w,*), the *d* is also voiced and is thus pronounced as we usually pronounce *d*. After unvoiced consonants (*ch, f, k, p, s, sh, x*), the *ed* is pronounced like *t*.

About fifty commonly used verbs are irregular in the past tense. A few of them, like *put, set,* and *knit,* are the same in the past affirmative statement as in the present, except in the third person singular, which does not add an *s* as it does in the present. The past of the question is formed by using *did* instead of *do* or *does.* The past of the negative uses *did not* or *didn't* instead of its *do* counterparts. After the *did* in both the question and the negative forms, the simple form of the verb is used.

The perfect is formed with the auxiliary verb *have* plus the past participle. The affirmative statement is formed with *have/has/had* between the subject and the participle. Placing *not* after or attaching *n't* to the auxiliary forms the negative. The question is formed by reversing the subject and the auxiliary. *He has eaten his lunch. He has not/ hasn't eaten his lunch. Has he eaten his lunch?*

Where there are no auxiliary verbs, verbs combine with "to" between them or by adding *ing* to the second, as in *I like to swim* or *I hate shopping.* That's it. Understanding how to use these inflections and auxiliary verbs is roughly the equivalent of knowing all 70 forms of the Spanish verb.

Students need to understand when to use which tense, but it is not necessary to give them every application of a tense when they learn it. The present progressive is generally used to express action at this very moment, but this is not always the case. *I am reading a good book* can mean that I am reading it at this moment, or that I have started a book and intend to finish it, or that I will read it in the near future. When you introduce the present progressive, it is sufficient to provide a single application. Once the structure is mastered, you can explain others.

PRONOUN CASES

Pity the poor students of German when they study nouns. Before choosing an article, they must determine if a noun is masculine, feminine, neuter, singular, plural, genitive, dative ... and so on. In English, different genders do not call for different articles, and we have cases only for pronouns.

I, you, he, she, it, we, and *they* are subject pronouns. *Me, you, him, her, it, us,* and *them* are object pronouns. You need only explain that the subject pronoun is placed before the verb and object pronoun is placed after, as in the sentences, *He sees me* or *We know them.* The only exception is when a form of *to be* is used as the copula, in which case only the subject form is used, as in *Who is he?* or *It is I.* Of course, most native speakers prefer the more commonly used but incorrect *It's me.*

The possessive pronouns are *my, your, his, her, its, our,* and *their,* and *mine, yours, his, hers, ours,* and *theirs.* Those in the first set are really adjectives that must precede the nouns they modify, while the second are true pronouns that stand alone.

With the exception of *himself* and *themselves,* the reflexive pronouns are the same as the possessive with *self* attached to the singular and *selves* attached to the plural (*myself, yourself, himself, herself, itself, ourselves, yourselves, themselves*).

IMPLICIT AND EXPLICIT GRAMMAR INSTRUCTION

Learning grammar is a bit like learning chess. One can learn the moves in a few hours, but it takes months or years to master the game. In like fashion, you can explain the rules of grammar in an hour or two, and your students can memorize them in a few weeks, but it will probably take a year or more before they can apply most of them automatically. As Erasmus discovered five centuries ago, the implicit and the explicit can work together.

We hear stories about people who studied vocabulary and grammar for several years and seemed to learn nothing, yet became reasonably fluent after living a few months where the language is spoken. It is not that those years in class were wasted. Inert knowledge can become active with practice. All contact with English serves to reinforce grammar lessons, but specific activities can help students to learn to apply grammar rules automatically. You may choose to do some of these activities first and reserve the explicit grammar explanations for later.

PATTERN PRACTICE MAKES PERFECT: WELL, NOT REALLY, BUT IT WORKS

Pattern practice can be useful as long as you know when to break the pattern. Many textbooks employ written pattern exercises, but pattern practice can be done orally as well. Model a sentence and then give students a cue to modify it. Patterns such as *I run, you run, he runs* oblige students to apply the third-person-singular rule. Say one of the sentences and then point to different people or groups of people and have a student provide the appropriate sentence. Patterns like *Today I work, yesterday I worked, tomorrow I will work* help students practice tenses. Model one of these sentences and cue by pointing to different dates on the calendar. Patterns can drill more than one concept at a time. *I have a motorcycle, but I don't have a car—She has a motorcycle, but she doesn't have a car* requires students to form compound sentences and practice the present tense in both the affirmative and the negative. Cue by nodding or shaking your head as you point to students and objects.

Exposure to patterns is useful, even before students are able to make conversions, especially if the patterns are fun. Carolyn Graham's *Jazz Chants* offer pattern practice in a form that most students find agreeable. A mix of clever lyrics and background music is the spoonful of sugar that helps the medicine go down. I strongly recommend *Jazz Chants for Children*, even for secondary students. The chants found in the book and accompanying tape cover the entire range of key English structures, and most students find them amusing. All of the *Jazz Chant* books are good, but some make some references to adult situations, like drinking alcoholic beverages, and therefore are not appropriate for classes with minors.

GRAMMAR IN ACTION: QUESTIONS, ANSWERS, JOKES, AND CONVERSATION

Controlled conversations in which students are obliged to make verb conversions drill grammar while approximating real-life use of language. If you are fortunate enough to have reasonably small classes, ask students questions that oblige them to convert the verb to a different form. *Where do you study? Where does your sister study? What did you study yesterday? When will you study for the test?*

You can evoke negative responses by asking students absurd questions. *Do you eat cockroaches? Do you sleep in the bathtub? Does your brother wear a tie around his leg?* When students are ready, it is a good idea to mix yes/no questions with "wh" questions. *Do you live in a shoe? (No, I don't live in a shoe.) Where do you live? (I live in an apartment.) Who lives in a shoe? (The old lady in the nursery rhyme with all the kids lives in a shoe.)*

Early in the course, students will want to answer questions with only a word or two, or perhaps with only gestures. This is acceptable during the first few months of study. After that period, however, students should be required to answer in complete, correct sentences at least part of the time. This will help them to gain command of the structures they will need to communicate effectively in the English language.

There are many ways to evoke questions and commands. You may have students ask other students questions or give them commands. *Ask him where he lives. Ask her if she is from Argentina. Ask them when they eat breakfast. Ask us what we ate for lunch. Tell Fulano to stand up. Tell Maria to tell us a joke. Tell Ngyuen to ask Mai if she likes her English class.*

My favorite way of evoking questions in the past tense is with *What did I do?*, a technique taken from a Carolyn Graham *Jazz Chant*. The teacher or a student makes an accusation, such as *You ruined it*, and another student responds, *What did I ruin*? or *He stole it*, with the response *What did he steal*? or *You offended her*, with the response, *Whom did I offend*?

TAG, YOU'RE IT: CONVERTING STATEMENTS INTO TAG QUESTIONS

Students can learn a lot about grammar by converting statements into tag questions. Tag questions are created by adding final tags such as *will you? have I? does he? did you? are they? hasn't he?* or *can't we?* to statements. Their formation is not as simple as it may seem to native speakers of English. Affirmative statements require negative tags, while negative statements require affirmative tags. The affirmative statement *You are happy* requires the negative tag *aren't you?* whereas the negative *You aren't happy* requires the affirmative tag *are you*? Statements with modals require the same modal in the tag. *He can't lift that* calls for the tag *can he? They should study harder* calls for the tag *shouldn't they?* The forms of *to be* and the auxiliary forms of *have* also are repeated in the tags. *The weather is nice* requires the tag *isn't it. Yumiko hasn't been to school this week* requires the tag *has she?* Other statements require a form of "do" in the tag. *We work too hard* takes the tag *don't we? That computer didn't work yesterday* requires the tag *did it?* Once students understand that *You like your English class* requires the tag *don't you?* while *You're not Argentine* requires the tag *are you?*, they have a pretty fair understanding of the English verb.

In like manner, students learn appropriate structures by practicing appropriate short answers. *Do you speak English?* calls for the answer *I do*, while the question *Are you in the United States?* calls for the answer *I am*. Once students have mastered those most magic of little words *is, am, are, was, were, can, could, should, would, might, must, may, will, shall, do, does, did, have, has,* and *had*, they are well on their way.

Working With Younger Students

Although the study of grammatical rules when mixed with other language-learning activities can enhance language learning among older students, the explicit study of grammar is, for most younger children, a waste of time. In the first place, they will not understand the rules. In the second, they will not need them. Young children absorb rules more easily than they comprehend them. Pattern practices, at least the fun ones like Graham's *Jazz Chants*, are effective ways to speed their absorption of the rules of grammar. Controlled conversation is also effective for all ages. With the very young, it is better to model grammar than to explain it.

9

Listening Skills

The Gateway to Language

O f the four language skills—listening, speaking, reading, and writing—listening is the most used and hence the most important. It is also arguably the easiest to learn. Not easy, mind you, just easier than the others. Listening involves a great deal of mental activity. Still, those in the early stages of language learning can understand much more than they can say. Even native speakers readily understand certain words that do not easily come to mind.

Again, it is best to not require beginning ESL students to speak during the first month or two of class, although those who choose to speak should be allowed and encouraged to do so. Do, however, demand interaction. You can do a lot of Total Physical Response (TPR) and ask a lot of questions that can be answered with gestures or with a few simple words. You can ask, "Where is the window?" or "It's too hot. What should I open?" to which the student may respond by either saying "the window" or by pointing to a window. You can ask questions that students can answer either by saying "Yes" or "No," or by nodding or shaking their heads.

Speak in complete sentences much of the time but in such a manner that your students can understand your meaning by identifying familiar key words within those sentences. If you say, "Please open your textbook to page twelve," students who only understand the words "open" and "twelve" will probably be able to understand what you want them to do, especially if it is about the time that students usually open their books. If not, repeat the request while opening a book and pointing to the number 12.

When practical, it is a good idea to control your vocabulary so that your students understand most of what you say. Use gestures, objects, pictures, or context clues to make your meaning clear. It is *not*, however, necessary for your students to understand all of what they hear in the early stages of language learning. Although much of the language that you provide should be, as USC professor emeritus Steven Krashen says, comprehensible input, there will be no harm if students are exposed to language that goes over their heads. During the first year or two of study, much of what your students hear outside your classroom will be difficult for them to understand, and they should learn early on to not be intimidated by the incomprehensible. Remember that any contact with the target language serves a purpose. Even when students appear to understand nothing, their subconscious minds are picking up bits and pieces that blend into the pot of language that they learn both in and out of your class.

LEARNING WITH A TAPE RECORDER OR CD PLAYER

The simple tape player and its modern sibling the CD player have been incredible boons to language teachers and learners. Recorded tapes or audio CDs work very well for teaching listening skills. There are all kinds of available taped materials with dialogues, songs, stories, and so forth. Several ESL textbooks come with accompanying tapes or CDs. Recorded lessons offer students unlimited exposure to spoken English while away from the classroom. Now that portable cassette players are available for less than $20, almost any student can afford one.

One hour per day spent listening to repeated dialogues or stories goes a long way for a student who has little opportunity for exposure to English outside of school. Five hours goes even farther. Do not let your students settle for listening to each tape only a time or two. Ten times is good, 20 is better, and 100 may not be too many for students who are having difficulties. A 10-hour taped English course contains enough language to allow a student to function reasonably well among native speakers. A student who listens for one hour per day for a year can hear each lesson in such a course almost 40 times. Most people spend more than one hour per day walking around, standing in line, or doing simple chores during which time they could listen to tapes.

If you have never studied a language with tapes, get a taped language course and practice on yourself. Avoid the phrasebook tapes with side-by-side oral translations. They are designed for tourists, not serious language learners. Find tapes with only the target language, but with accompanying written materials in both the target language and English. Study the lesson, listen to the tape, read a translation or look up unfamiliar words, and repeat, repeat, repeat. You will be surprised how much you can learn as you jog, vacuum the floor, or shop for groceries.

LEARNING WITH SOFTWARE: THE ROSETTA STONE, INSTANT IMMERSION, AND OTHER PROGRAMS

Computer programs now exist that teach listening skills almost as well as one-to-one tutors. These programs begin by presenting objects, saying the word or phrase that identifies them, and then instructing the student to click on the object. Later in the program, students must follow more complex directions. Some even use this technique to teach question forms, complex sentences, and tenses. In such a program, the computer might display several objects—let's say a ball, a pencil, a book, and a coin—as it says the words. The student would then be asked to select the ball. A later lesson might ask the student to select a ball that is red, or to select the object that can be used to write. Later in the course, the computer might show pictures of someone about to jump, someone jumping, and someone who has just landed, and then ask the student to identify who will jump, who is jumping, and who jumped.

My personal favorite language-teaching computer program is *The Rosetta Stone*, although it is one of the most expensive. This is a fairly complete course that includes a comprehensive beginning vocabulary and key grammatical structures. You would not go wrong if you made *The Rosetta Stone* the central curriculum for a beginning class, providing that you supplemented it with other materials and activities. This is not true of most computer-based programs, but most are useful. Among the reasonably priced programs, *Instant Immersion* is good, but as a supplement rather than as the main course.

If you have good computer skills, you can mix scanned photos or pictures from a digital camera and sound files to create your own cyber-lessons to reinforce the lessons learned in your classroom. One caveat: Avoid computer programs that are little more than video worksheets. Such programs are not a total waste of time, but they do not make full use of a computer's language-teaching potential.

THE GREAT ESL FILM FESTIVAL

During at least the first few months of class, it is a good idea to show a number of English movies. Students enjoy them, and they provide quite a bit of contact with English. This activity also helps encourage students to begin "studying" English at home on their own television sets.

Even though beginning students will understand almost none of the language in an English language film, it is important that they focus on what they hear. One way to get this focus is to give them several words to "hunt." Present, define, and drill the words and then offer a small prize or some sort of recognition to those who first raise their hands upon hearing one of those words. Limit each student to a set number of guesses, perhaps one per scene or three per film. If you do not include such a rule, some of your students will be venturing wild guesses every few seconds. At the very first, you might want to limit the hunt to greetings, numbers, and place names. Later, you can pick words that will be repeated often in the film. For *The Wizard of Oz*, for example, you might ask students to hunt for the following words: Dorothy, Kansas, storm, yellow, west, slippers, scarecrow, tin, lion, and balloon. For *Cinderella*, you could use kingdom, ugly, prince, stepsister, mouse, ball, and slipper.

It is also helpful to provide a brief synopsis of each movie in the students' native language before they view it, so that they can follow the thread of the plot even through sections they do not understand. As students become more advanced, you can use films to present information, to reinforce vocabulary and structures, and as a springboard for class discussions.

DICTATION

Dictation, in which teachers speak and students copy the words exactly as spoken, is a valuable tool for teaching not only writing but listening as well. To correctly take dictation, students must know not only how to spell a word, but also how to recognize its sounds. Early in the course you can help students learn to identify English words and sounds with number dictations. Because our number system is pretty much universal, all but the youngest students should be prepared for this activity. Once students can understand a few hundred words, you can do a pre-dictation activity in which the teacher speaks and the students draw pictures depicting what the teacher describes. Once your students have some English writing skills, you can have them write your exact words. There will be more about dictation in Chapter 12.

ENCOURAGING LISTENING
AS A STAND-ALONE SKILL

It is best that students do not see the written word in the early stages of language study. People do not come with speech balloons. It takes some time and practice to learn to identify the sounds of a foreign language. Some students who begin reading and listening together come to use the text as a crutch, and this may interfere with learning to hear and differentiate English sounds. For students who know the Roman alphabet, it is easier to recognize an English word that is seen than one that is heard. It is better, however, for beginning students to tough it out for the first two months or so and learn to identify the new sounds of English as they hear them.

Early dependence on the written word can also result in bad speaking habits. Consider the following example. The sound of the English short *o* exists in Spanish, but it is written with the letter *a*. The Spanish *o* is similar to the English long *o*, so many native speakers of Spanish pronounce the English word "not" like "note," even after they have become fluent English speakers. This is because they had let reading get ahead of oral language. It is better to wait until students have been exposed to all of the sounds in English and can make some sense of the English they hear before they start their reading lessons. Once they have mastered the English sound system, they can then learn written and oral language together. If students are to spend three years or more mastering English, it is not unreasonable to allot the first two months of study to listening skills only.

TEACHING WITH MINIMAL PAIRS: BIT, BET, BAIT, BEET, BITE

Some students, especially older ones, will have trouble distinguishing English sounds, even after much contact with oral English. For such students, sound recognition can be drilled with minimal pair exercises. Many English learners have trouble distinguishing between the words *bet* and *bit*, or between *ship* and *sheep*, or between *ban* and *van*. You can help them train their ears by presenting the words and having them choose which you said.

After your students begin to read, you can write similar words on opposite sides of the chalkboard and have them point to the appropriate word as you say it. Another way is to mix the words and have students count. Say, *"Bit, bet, bit, bit, bet"* and ask them to count *bit*. You may then add other similar words, like *bait, beet,* and *bite.* After your students begin to write, you can dictate paired words, either in isolation or embedded in short sentences.

You can make minimal pair practice amusing by having students identify pictures as you describe them. Show a picture of a chambermaid making a bed and a person bidding at an auction and then ask, "Who is making a bed?" and "Who is making a bid?" Or show a picture of a child riding a sheep and another of a sailor on the deck of a ship. Ask "Who is on a sheep?" and "Who is on a ship?" Many of your students, especially the younger ones, will learn to differentiate English sounds without drills.

For them, pair drills will be counterproductive, or at least a waste of time. Save these drills for the second semester, and use them with only those students who need them.

Working With Younger Students

Taped language courses are of little use for small children. Tapes with English songs, stories, or rhymes, however, will be useful. There are some good computer English language courses designed specifically for young children. Although nominally a Spanish course, *Jump Start Spanish* can be set to teach English. This program covers a vocabulary of only about 100 words, but children love it. It is not normally necessary to teach minimal pairs to young children. With enough exposure to the language, they will learn to distinguish sounds on their own.

10

Now Say It

Teaching Spoken English

Of the four language skills—listening, speaking, reading, and writing—speaking is the most difficult to teach to large groups. Twenty-five students can listen to one teacher, but only one can speak to the teacher at one time. Students learn to speak by speaking. If classes are large, it is difficult to provide them opportunities to do so. The ideal situation for teaching speaking skills is one-on-one tutoring. Of course, few language teachers have that luxury.

THE DIRECT METHOD

For those with small classes or lots of volunteer help, some techniques from the direct method work very well. Variations of the direct method have worked very well for private language companies, many of which claim this method as their own, calling it the (add company name here) method. Business people and travelers who need a command of a new language quickly will pay handsomely for this sort of instruction delivered in a one-on-one setting. The direct method shares much with the natural approach. Both stress extensive use of the target language in the classroom, although the direct method calls for earlier speech and greater attention paid to structure.

CONTROLLED CONVERSATION

The direct method includes controlled conversation. With this technique, students can do most of the talking while teachers guide conversation so that students practice appropriate structures and vocabulary. It is easy for teachers or tutors to learn this technique, so it is an appropriate method to use with volunteer peers or adult tutors.

After you demonstrate an action, describe it. As you jump, say "I am jumping." Then ask the student to jump and say, "You are jumping." Then repeat the action and ask the student to describe it. If you ask, "What am I doing?" the student can respond, "You are jumping." If the student responds incorrectly, provide the correct response and ask again.

When the student is comfortable giving a descriptive response, go on to yes-and-no questions. Begin with the affirmative: "Is he jumping?" "Is she jumping?" while pointing to students who are jumping. After the student is comfortable giving affirmative answers, model the negative: "Is she jumping?" "No, she is not jumping. She is sitting." Then ask the student a question that calls for a negative response.

When students are comfortable responding in the negative, direct them to ask the questions. This technique also works well with small groups. You can ask student A to tell student B to open the door. Then tell student C to ask student D what student B is doing, and so on.

It is a good idea to have controlled-conversation parallel listening activities or memorized pattern practice, although not necessarily at the same time. Even after students pass the silent period, some, but not all, do better if a week or two passes between listening activities and similar speaking activities based on a given structure or set of vocabulary. If students can learn to produce a structure orally as soon as they can under-stand it, by all means do nothing to hold them back. Those who require an incubation period between listening and speaking, however, should be allowed one.

If your textbook presents grammatical structures sequentially, have your students practice them with controlled conversation. This technique also works well with Carolyn Graham's *Jazz Chants*. After students memorize a chant, or any pattern exercise, controlled conversation will help lead them toward applying that structure actively.

ROLE PLAYING

Role playing is a good way to help your students acquire survival-level English speaking skills. You can role play trips to the doctor, shopping trips, going through customs, and so forth. You can preview key words for the role play with Total Physical Response (TPR), word lists, or demon-strations. Once students pass the survival level, you can make role playing more challenging by changing the hypothetical situations. Intermediate students could take the roles of a police officer and a driver who tries to talk his way out of a traffic ticket, or a department store clerk and a customer who wants to return defective merchandise. Advanced students could take the parts of a company executive and a union representative negotiating a new contract or a helpdesk technician and a computer user whose system has just crashed.

STUDENT-TO-STUDENT TEACHING

If your classes are large you might want to have your students break up into groups and practice speaking with one another. Be warned, however, that unless your students are self-motivated and self-directed, such sessions might become a waste of time. They might revert to a lot of repetition of what the students already know or even become gossip sessions in the students' native language. If you teach ESL to a linguistically heterogeneous group, you can avoid the latter problem by matching students with partners with different native languages. In any event, monitor the conversations and nudge them toward challenging levels.

One way to monitor such classes is to require the students to produce something. You can give one student a picture or object to describe and then require the other student or students to draw it from the English description. Or you can have a student explain how to put together a puzzle, assemble a model, set up a computer program, or do a magic trick, and then ask listeners to do the task based only on their classmate's oral directions.

RECITALS

Allow your students the opportunity to show what they know in front of the class. A recital can be something as simple as a dialogue or a role play, or as complicated as a soliloquy from a Shakespeare play. With advanced students, you might even have students stage a one-act play in English. In the case of extremely shy students, use your best judgment before demanding recitals.

USING MEDIA AND THE LANGUAGE LABORATORY

Thirty years ago language laboratories were standard equipment in high school language classes. As the audiolingual method fell out of fashion, these labs disappeared. The labs could not match a good human teacher working with a small group, but they were good for large class instruction or for independent study. Students would listen to the target language and repeat or respond into a microphone. Usually the material matched the lessons in the textbook. Students could hear their own words through headphones as they said them and later hear them played back alongside the words of a native speaker. The teacher or a monitor could cut in to listen to individual students as they spoke or check tapes of a student's speech later.

Like the language labs, a great many computer-based language programs, even some of the inexpensive ones, allow students to record their voices and compare their words to those of native speakers. Some of these programs include voice recognition software that will rate the quality of the speaker's accent, but, at the time of this writing, such software is still imperfect.

If language labs or computers are not available, students can use tape recorders or video cameras to achieve the same end. They can simply listen to a taped lesson, record themselves, and then listen to the tapes side by side.

TEACHING PRONUNCIATION

Some students, particularly the young ones, will learn to pronounce English well through mimicry alone. Others will need more help. In the case of pronunciation, it is best to not start at the beginning. Rather, wait until several months into the course when students are communicating orally to determine who needs this sort of instruction. It is not necessary to remove all traces of a foreign accent, but it is important that speech be intelligible.

Teachers who speak their students' language have an advantage in this matter. Many sounds, called *allophones*, are not considered phonemes in a language but exist as parts of phonemes or variants of phonemes. Although students in beginning Spanish class learn that there are only five Spanish vowel sounds, this is not strictly true. Actually, the equivalent of the English short *i* and *e* exist in Spanish. In polysyllabic words, the unaccented *i* or *e* are pronounced like their English counterparts. While the *ch* sound in English does not exist in Spanish (the Spanish *ch* is somewhere between the English *sh* and *ch*), a Spanish speaker asked to read *tch* will pronounce the English *ch* perfectly.

For students who still struggle with sounds that do not exist in their native language, you may need to explain where the points of articulation are so that they can consciously place their tongues or lips where they need to be. Consciously placing the tongue is tedious and can interfere with communication at first. With practice, however, proper placement will become automatic. A good bilingual dictionary will explain where these points of articulation are, as will some textbooks. If you do not speak the students' language, learn its points of articulation as well. Sometimes a letter may represent sounds that are similar but not exactly the same in the two languages. Your school's speech therapist could be helpful in this matter.

USING THE INTERNATIONAL PHONETIC ALPHABET

The International Phonetic Alphabet (IPA) can be of great help in learning to pronounce English. Most bilingual dictionaries use it, so a student who knows the IPA has the tools necessary to pronounce words without asking an English speaker for help. For those who still have difficulty producing certain English sounds after several months of English study, IPA transcription can be useful. Write transcriptions of your students' speech in regular script accompanied by a phonetic transcription that exactly mirrors his or her pronunciation. You can then point out which sounds are troublesome and, if need be, drill them.

ERROR CORRECTION: WHEN AND HOW OFTEN

It will not be wise to attempt to correct every error your students make. The nature of language learning is such that your students will make literally hundreds of thousands of errors before fully mastering English. It will prove impossible to correct more than a few of them. Egos can be fragile, and you do not want to dampen the enthusiasm of a child who finally worked up the nerve to ask you a question in English by pointing out that the question contained seven errors. On the other hand, repeated errors may fossilize and become a permanent part of a student's speech, particularly for beginning students who are in or beyond adolescence, and you want the students to repair those errors before they become permanent, flawed parts of their language.

In the early stages of language learning, new speakers will rely on what linguists call *interlanguage*. Sometimes interlanguage will be English vocabulary paired with the structure of the student's native language, or it might be based on structures that the student invents. A student who does not understand how to correctly form the negative in English might say "I no have pencil." One who does not understand pronoun cases might say "Me no have pencil" or "Me pencil not." Speaking in interlanguage is better than not speaking at all, so encourage any early efforts to communicate in English, flawed as they might be. After the student has gained a bit of confidence, begin to correct prudently. It is not necessary to say "No, it's 'I don't have a pencil'" over and over. It is better to occasionally remind the student, in private if necessary, of the proper structure. Once the student understands the correct structure, respond to the error by raising your eyebrows and waiting for a self-correction.

LET YOUR STUDENTS CORRECT YOU, TOO

If you speak the students' native language imperfectly, do not become angry when they correct you. To do so would contradict the message that making and correcting errors is a normal part of the language-learning process. Do, however, insist that they follow the same procedure for correcting your errors that you use for theirs. Do not allow them to interrupt you when you are speaking to the class, but encourage them to note the error and bring it to your attention at an appropriate time.

SPEAKING PRACTICE OUTSIDE OF CLASS

If a community has few speakers of the students' language, real life will provide your students with both the opportunity and the obligation to speak. If not, the amount of speaking practice that your students get will vary greatly. Some of your students will have English-speaking friends and relatives. The more gregarious ones will strike up conversations even with strangers. Some, however, will speak little English outside of your classroom. All ESL students should spend part of their school day among native speakers, at least for classes like art and physical education, but some will avoid their English-speaking peers, even if they spend a lot of time in the mainstream. For those who haven't made English-speaking friends by the end of the first semester, try to arrange for assigned "buddies" or tutors who can engage them in conversation before and after school, or between classes. Remember that one learns to speak by speaking, and that speech is only meaningful when there is a listener.

Working With Younger Students

Young children love to play pretend, so the possibilities for role playing are endless. You will not have to worry about showing points of articulation to most young students. Given enough time and exposure to a language, most young children can learn accent-free speech with mimicry alone. Although you may want to correct your students' errors, keep in mind that small children's errors are not likely to fossilize as older students' might.

11

English in Black and White

Teaching Reading

It is a good idea to wait two or three months before introducing students to the written English word. Again, for students who have trouble distinguishing English sounds, early reliance on the written English word can become a crutch that will hinder the development of skills essential to listening.

There is a myth that it is easier to learn to read and write a language than to speak it. This myth is perpetuated by people who have been caught orally struggling with a language that they have studied and profess to know. If you know the language that such a nonspeaking reader claims to understand, produce a novel and ask for an explanation of a passage with which you have been struggling. You will likely discover that "reading well" is little more than picking out cognates.

There probably really are people in the world who really have learned to read and write a language well without having first learned to understand the spoken word, perhaps in insular dictatorships like China in the era of the Red Guard and Enver Hoxa's Albania, but their number is certainly small. I have never met one. Both research and experience indicate that reading and writing best follow, or at least parallel, listening and speaking. Do not be seduced by the false hope that your students will bypass oral language and still become competent readers.

WHEN STUDENTS ARE STRUGGLING READERS IN THEIR NATIVE LANGUAGE

Once students are familiar with the new sound system and are able to understand spoken English, at least at a basic level, they will be ready to begin reading English. At this point it is extremely important to know where students are academically. It will be pointless to teach students who are not competent readers in their native tongues at the same pace as those who can read at least one language at or above grade level.

Teachers whose classes include a mix of readers and nonreaders really should have aides or the assistance of a remedial reading teacher. If such assistance is not available, the teacher should teach reading on at least two tracks. Teachers with students who attended little or no school in their native countries may want to write individual education programs (IEPs) for them. This is not easy, but sometimes a teacher has to make the best of difficult situations.

English learners who are poor readers or nonreaders in their native language have a double burden: to learn a foreign language and to master literacy skills. Such students should not be expected to read much beyond their oral vocabularies until they have become literate. Therefore, offer them a lot of oral language and follow up with reading at the same level.

Students who are literate in their native languages are another matter completely. Literacy skills do transfer between languages, so literate students armed with bilingual dictionaries will be able to read English that is somewhat beyond their listening level.

QUICK-START PHONICS FOR ENGLISH LEARNERS

It is not necessary to reinvent the wheel. Students who already know the Roman alphabet will not need to review every letter and rule. Even those who use different writing systems have the skill of matching symbol to sound or meaning. Find out how the English writing system varies from that of your students and teach only that which is necessary.

Students whose languages are written with script other than the Roman may still know the Roman alphabet. Japanese students learn our alphabet at an early age. Roman letters are used in Japanese writing for certain special purposes, like the call letters of radio and television stations. In some Chinese-speaking countries, young children learn to read basic words of their own language phonetically with our alphabet before learning to read the more difficult Chinese characters. Students who have studied a bit of English in their native countries will probably have learned our ABCs. Such students, however, will need more practice with our writing system than will those whose languages employ Roman script. There is a big difference between mere passing familiarity and the mastery that comes with years of daily contact.

There are actually more than 200 spelling conventions in English, although many of them are obscure and used in only a few words. Because this book is a quick-start manual, we will deal only with the most important ones. Once your students reach the point where they can read words that follow the most common conventions, you can introduce students to the less common ones. A number of good spelling and reading books provide this information.

The good news is that about 80% of all that children say, read, and write consists of a mere 1,000 basic words. And there is more good news. Although English has one of the least phonetic spelling systems, about 85% of the words follow common spelling conventions. *Ergo*, if a page has 300 words, readers whose listening vocabulary is adequate for the text and whose sight word vocabulary includes the basic thousand words will be able to read 240 of them. If they know the basic rules of phonics, they will be able to decode 51 of the remaining 60 words, thus leaving a mere nine words that cannot be read. Context clues may clarify a few more. The six or seven words per page that our reader cannot decode will still be a challenge, but hardly an insurmountable one.

THE CONSTANT CONSONANTS

Consonants, for the most part, are constant. Only *c, g, h, w,* medial and final *s,* and medial *t* have more than one sound. *C* is soft like an unvoiced *s* when it is found before an *e, i,* or *y*. In other cases it is hard like a *k*. The *g* is sometimes soft like a *j* when it is found before an *e, i,* or *y*. Final *g* is always hard, and final *ge* is always soft. Before *a, o, u,* or any consonant, the *g* is always hard, except when it is silent or part of a diagraph. *W* and *h* are sometimes silent. Initial *k* and *g* are silent when found before an *n*. Medial and final *s* may be voiced like a *z* or unvoiced, or it may be pronounced as it is in *measure*. The medial *t* may be pronounced with a flap of the tongue, like the medial Spanish *r*. *C, g, w, s,* and *t* may be combined with other letters to form the diagraphs *ch, gh, wh, sh,* and *th*. While *p* only has one sound by itself, it appears in the diagraph *ph*.

If your students read Spanish, it will be a simple matter to teach them the English consonants. Only the Spanish consonants *g, h, j, q, ll, r, x,* and *z* differ much from those of English. Some other letters differ slightly, but this is a matter of pronunciation, not reading. Most English diagraphs do not exist in Spanish. Of our consonant diagraphs, only *ch* exists, although it is not pronounced exactly the same. *Sh, ph, rh, gh,* and *wh* will be unfamiliar to Spanish speakers who are just beginning to study English.

Consonant blends may prove tricky for your students. Some languages have no consonant blends. Others lack some blends that are common in English. In Spanish, for example, the blend *sc* does not exist. When *s* and *c* are encountered together there is a syllable break between them, as in *escuela* (pronounced *es quay-la*). For this reason, a Spanish speaker might pronounce *school* as *es-cool*.

THOSE TRICKY VOWELS

English vowels are trickier than consonants. English has the misfortune to have 17 vowels and diphthongs and only 6 letters with which to represent them (7 if you count the unsung semivowel *w*). In the majority of cases, the vowels are long or short. The short vowels are all pure vowels, while the long vowels are all diphthongs of two pure vowel sounds. Generally the long vowel diphthong is represented by the same letter as the short vowel, with a silent vowel following to indicate that the previous vowel is long. This is confusing to speakers of languages like Spanish in which each letter representing a vowel sound is pronounced.

In grade school, those of us who learned to read with phonics learned the rule, "When two vowels go walking, the first one does the talking." Usually a pair of vowels indicates that the first vowel is long and the second is silent. An *e* at the end of a word is also usually silent and indicates that the previous vowel is long. We also learned that the vowels in open syllables are generally long, while those in closed syllables are generally short. It is easiest to explain the open/closed syllable rule thus: Two or more consonants in a row—either the same, as in *miller*, or different, as in *banter*—usually indicate that the previous vowel is short. A single medial consonant, as in *cutest* or *filing*, indicates that the previous vowel is long.

Many words that English borrowed from Romance languages (French, Spanish, Italian) preserve the Romance pronunciation of vowels. Many words that end in vowels other than *e* follow this convention.

Although the short vowels are pretty consistent, there are several conventions for the long ones. There are seven common ways to represent the long *a*. Three follow the vowels-walking-and-talking rule, as in *trail, fame,* and *play*. Two are irregular, as in *they* and *weight*. One follows the open/closed syllable rule, as in *aping* or *debater*. In words borrowed from Romance languages, the long *a* sound may be represented by *e*, as in *cafe* or *quesadilla*.

There are seven common ways to represent the long *e*. Three follow the walking-talking vowel rule, as in *cede, real,* and *feet*. The final *y* may be pronounced as a long *e*, as in *candy*, as can *ie*, as in *Barbie, rabies,* or *thief*. *E* before a single consonant is usually long, as in *meter*. In words borrowed from Romance languages, the long *e* sound may be represented with *i*, as in *piano* or *spaghetti*.

There are five common conventions for the long *i* sound. Two follow the walking, talking rule, as in *file* and *lie*. One follows the open syllable convention, as in *spider*. Two are irregular, as in *sigh* and *dry*.

There are six common conventions for the long *o*. Four follow the walking, talking vowel convention, as in *pole, soap, hoe,* and *know. O* also often becomes long before *r* or *l*, as in *fold* or *for. O* is generally long before a single consonant, as in *motion*.

There are two ways to pronounce the long *u*, as in *mute* and *fruit*. There are six common conventions for writing the long *u* sound. Three follow the walking, talking vowel convention, as with *cute, cue,* and *fruit*. One follows the open syllable rule, as in *futile* or *ruler*. Two are irregular, as in *crew* and *boot*.

There are special diphthongs and vowel diagraphs that are neither long vowels nor the sum of the letters that represent them. They are *au, aw, oo, ou,* and *oi*.

Many English learners find the schwa sound tricky. If they have difficulty pronouncing it, tell them that it is much like the sound one makes upon being hit in the stomach. In many English polysyllabic words, the vowel in the syllable with the least accent, be it *a, e, i, o,* or *u,* will take the schwa sound. Generally a syllable with a long vowel will take the primary accent, turning the vowel in at least one other syllable into a schwa, as in *furious* (schwa in the third syllable), *chromosome* (schwa in the second), and *supply* (schwa in the first). The extent to which the schwa is used varies from region to region and from person to person.

It is a good idea to present these rules at least a month before your students start reading for comprehension. Students can begin by practicing reading single words from the board or flashcards for a few minutes each day. Spelling pairs can be used to present new reading rules. Show the students *cot* and *coat, can* and *cane, bit* and *bite, mull* and *mule, miller* and *miler, licking* and *liking, beating* and *betting,* and *cutter* and *cuter* to emphasize the representations of the sounds. You can steadily increase the time dedicated to flashcard and pair reading by a few minutes each week for six weeks or so; then begin reading from texts.

DECODING SKILLS
AND BACKGROUND KNOWLEDGE

You might want to begin having your students read common irregular words about this time. As with speaking, there are a few hundred key words that readers encounter scores or even hundreds of times in a single day. Many commercial packages provide lists of these words and products to teach them. The best known is the Dolch word list, a list of 220 essential sight words chosen for young readers. An abundance of material based on Dolch words is available.

You might be tempted to bypass phonics and teach sight words only. Bear in mind, however, that your students will probably not be able to learn the thousands of words that they need by sight only. Native speakers sometimes learn to read without mastering the rules of phonics by instead identifying the consonants and divining the rest of the word from its context. This is possible for someone who has a native speaker's oral vocabulary. New English learners, however, will not know many of the words they see and, rather than learning the new word, they might assume it to be one that is a part of their limited existing vocabulary.

Schema

Background knowledge is a huge part of reading. If readers do not have sufficient knowledge to understand a passage, even if their decoding skills and vocabulary are adequate, the passage will not make sense. A discussion of the effect that Roman rule had on ancient Britain will mean little to a student who knows nothing of the Roman Empire or ancient Britain. A student who knows nothing of cellular biology will not understand a description of mitosis. *Uncle Tom's Cabin* will make no sense to a reader who does not understand that at one time it was legal for one human being to own another. If you are an American and a baseball fan, you will probably have little difficulty understanding a sports writer's account of a Yankees and Red Sox game. You probably would, however, have great difficulty understanding an account of a cricket match.

When students are still struggling with decoding skills, avoid text that requires much background knowledge that your students lack. When students who can decode lack the background necessary to understand a passage, provide as much as you can in prereading activities. When English learners begin regular reading, they are likely to encounter comprehensible text punctuated by incomprehensible text. It helps the learner if you can provide "roadmaps" to guide them through the incomprehensible parts.

If your classes are small or you have volunteers, you can provide such information as you go. In one-on-one or small-group reading lessons, you can explain new vocabulary and provide background information (schema) that the readers will need to know in order to understand the passage.

If students are reading independently, you can help them understand the text by providing an outline or brief summary of the story beforehand. That way, if a section of the passage is over the student's head, he or she will still be able to follow the thread of the story and get back on track after reaching text that is comprehensible once again.

Graphic Organizers

Graphic organizers may prove helpful. Charts, graphs, Venn diagrams, and so on may help older students follow that which they are about to read. Pictures illustrating what they are about to read, combined with explanations and definitions, can be helpful prereading activities.

Working With Younger Students

If you are teaching very young children who are in a bilingual program, your students will be learning to read in their native language. If this is the case, it would be wise to emphasize spoken English until your students become reasonably competent readers in their first language. For young, preliterate children it is confusing to learn two sets of reading rules concurrently, especially if one system belongs to a language that they barely understand. After these students become literate in the primary language, be prepared to help them add English literacy to their skills.

If you teach preliterate students who are learning to read English only, do not expect them to outread their vocabularies. Those who have even a basic command of oral English can read primers, but a limited command of English will naturally limit English reading skills. As students' ability to understand oral English improve, they can move into more advanced reading. If students fall behind in reading because of incomplete mastery of English, be prepared to help them advance in literacy skills as their command of oral English improves.

12

Writing It Right

Teachers who begin with oral methods may become a bit less popular when the writing lessons begin. When the nice person with the toys, the movies, and the computer games produces a 100-word spelling/ vocabulary list each Monday, English class will not be quite as much fun for most of your students, but there will be exceptions. Some shy students and students who especially love the written word will begin to shine when they begin to write. The progression from speaking only to speaking and writing is necessary. If students are to learn to communicate in writing in one year and compete with native speakers in three, a lot of writing practice is necessary. The good news is that once your students see that they are becoming competent writers of English, your former popularity will be restored.

As with reading, there is a myth, perpetuated mostly by people who have studied languages without learning them particularly well, that one can learn to write a language without also learning to speak it. As with reading without listening, such an accomplishment might be possible, but I have yet to meet any truly competent writers of languages that they cannot speak. There are many people who write English well despite having accents that are difficult to understand. There are also nonspeakers who can expertly write form letters (i.e., Thank you for your order of . . . to be delivered to . . . on. . . .) but cannot write a coherent original composition. Do not expect to bypass speaking and go directly to writing. As with reading and listening, writing skills should follow or accompany speaking skills.

GETTING STARTED

Some teachers prefer to introduce English reading and writing together. I like to begin spelling lessons about a month after students begin to read and composition about a month after that. Most of my students like this arrangement, although some students prefer to begin reading and writing together. Reading and writing practice do reinforce one another, but many students are more comfortable with writing after they have had exposure to the written word through reading lessons.

WRITING BEGINS WITH SPELLING

Do not take the teaching of spelling lightly. Spelling is especially important for English learners. It is not uncommon for students to master oral English yet experience failure in academic classes simply because they cannot spell well enough to do the work required of them. As all of us know, English spelling is quirky. Even though English spelling is mostly rule governed, the many conventions and the large number of exceptions mean that students must memorize a great many of the words they will write. Even phonetically regular words may follow any of several conventions. Remember that there are seven "regular" ways to spell the long *a* sound.

Students who lack at least a fair command of English should not be forced to spell words they have not used, so begin with spelling/vocabulary words from their lessons. Spelling words can come from their textbooks, audiotapes, movies, and themed pages of picture dictionaries. Once students are able to handle English reasonably well, they will be ready to study spelling with a spelling book or computer program that presents words grouped according to spelling conventions. Do, however, incorporate these words into your lessons in other ways. Be certain that your students have the opportunity to also hear and say the words they are learning to write.

Again, a basic vocabulary of about 1,000 words makes up 80% of all that young people say and write, so students who can spell the basic thousand are off to a good start. At that point they should be able to write simple intelligible compositions with the help of dictionaries, assuming of course that they have an equivalent command of oral language. Except for students who cannot write their native language or those who do not use the Roman alphabet, most upper elementary and secondary students should be able to learn to spell beyond the basic thousand in their first year of English study.

Assuming that students begin their spelling lessons in the fourth month of the school year and they study 70 words per week for 24 weeks, they will cover 1,680 spelling words. A mere 60% mastery would give your students their basic thousand. Students who fail to learn to spell the basic thousand in the first year would be good candidates for summer school.

GADGETS AND MEDIA AGAIN

A number of good computer programs exist for teaching spelling. Spelling is one area in which programs designed for younger native speakers work well with English learners as well. Try out different spelling programs with your students and note both student response and results. Many good computer spelling programs mix spelling with games. Some, unfortunately, are more game than anything else. If you allow your students to study spelling with computer games, pay attention to which games yield the best results. Spelling tests scores will tell you which games are the most effective.

THE VANISHING WORD TECHNIQUE

Except for students who have not yet mastered the Roman alphabet, copying words over and over again is not a particularly efficient use of time. When students merely copy text, their minds are not obliged to remember. If, however, the students see the word for only a second or two and then it disappears before they begin to write, the mind must go to work. There are many ways to apply the vanishing word technique. You may write words on the board and then quickly erase or cover them, or you may present them on a television or computer screen using presentation software like Microsoft PowerPoint. Some computer spelling programs include activities that briefly display words on the screen and then require students to type from memory what they have seen. If you or someone in your school can program, you can make a vanishing word program with Microsoft Visual Basic or authoring software.

The vanishing word technique also works well as a paired activity. You can ask your students to copy their spelling words on note cards and then pair up. Students then can take turns briefly exposing words to their partners who will write them down. When they become more advanced, one student can briefly display two or three words and then ask the other student to compose a short sentence that includes them.

PICTURE AND WORD CARDS

For the spelling of concrete vocabulary words, you can purchase or create cards with pictures on one side and words on the other. The Frank Shaffer Company offers several sets of cards of this sort. Or you can ask students to make their own picture/word cards by taking note cards and writing on one side and drawing a picture on the other. Students can then study the words on their own by looking at the picture, writing the word or a sentence that includes the word, and turning over the card to check their spelling. This activity also helps students build their vocabularies.

PUNCTUATION AND CAPITALIZATION

If your students can write a language that employs the Roman alphabet, chances are that most of their knowledge of language mechanics will transfer to English. There will be some differences, however. For example, in Spanish capital letters are used at the beginning of sentences and for proper nouns, but not for days of the week or months, and only the first word of a title is capitalized. Although periods and commas are used in the same way in both languages, question marks and explanation points appear at both the beginning and end of interrogative and explanatory sentences, and direct quotations are punctuated differently.

DICTATION

The French, whose language has spelling that is at least as quirky as English, are fanatical about dictation. There is even an international contest called The Great Dictation in which a complicated passage is dictated and contestants write what they hear. Many participate each year but only a tiny handful produce perfect scores. I avoided giving dictations during my first few years as an ESL teacher because I hated the ones that I had to write in high school French class. Experience has since shown me that this technique is effective.

You can begin by dictating single words, and eventually work up to sentences, paragraphs, and even complete stories and essays. It is best to not ask your students to memorize the dictated passages beforehand, although most of the vocabulary used should have been already studied. Do not count as errors misspelled words that your students have not studied. You might want designate a few hundred Dolch or other basic words as "words you must never misspell," and count them as errors whenever you find them misspelled. This would be, of course, after students have had sufficient time to learn them. Some ESL computer programs have dictation features that allow students to hear a passage, type it, and then see errors displayed.

IN THEIR OWN WORDS

After the first semester or so, older students should be able to produce simple compositions and answer test questions with short sentences. At that point students can begin to practice independent writing in English by keeping journals, writing short narration, and communicating with pen pals, either by mail or over the Internet. Intermediate students can try their hands at creative writing. Few, if any, students will be able to write error-free in their first few years of English study.

Writing errors should be seen in the same light as errors in speech, an unavoidable part of learning a new language. Encourage your students to write in both your class and in their mainstream classes. Sometimes it is tempting to give English learners only true-false or multiple choice tests. Do not succumb to that temptation. Tests that require written answers oblige students to practice writing. As with speaking, correct the errors in vocabulary and structure that students have already studied. As they become independent writers, encourage them to use their dictionaries and word processors to correct spelling errors and enrich the vocabulary of their written work.

Of course, writing is more than talking on paper. Unlike informal speech, good writing is organized, terse, and efficient. Like many language skills, these writing skills will transfer from the native language. For those students who lack these skills, help build them. For those who have them, help hone them.

Working With Younger Students

With very young students, English writing will begin with the Roman alphabet. You can teach this skill to an English learner much as you would teach it to a native speaker. Some computer programs with spelling games are very effective with all young students. If you are working in a bilingual program, do not teach English and native language spelling at the same time until the students have become reasonably competent spellers in their native language. Young English learners can write original compositions in English, but do not demand that they write beyond their oral vocabularies.

13

How We Know What the Students Know

Grading and Testing

While we teachers are most concerned with student learning, some of those outside the classroom are more concerned with that graphic manifestation of learning, the grade. If many of your students fail, you might find yourself in the principal's office more often than your worst-behaved student. Parents who have never been to a PTA meeting or responded to a request to meet with you in your classroom will likely visit you for the first time when their children's grades drop below 70%. Sadly, you may be judged more by the grades you give than by the knowledge you impart. Whether you keep your job may depend more on how you grade than on how you teach.

GRADING IN MIXED-ABILITY CLASSROOMS

Because of the incredible range of backgrounds of students found in most ESL classes, it may be impossible to measure all students by the same standard. If a teacher sets a standard for written language that teen-age students who have attended only three years of school in their native countries can meet, the students who read and write their native language well will not be challenged. If the standard is appropriate for the latter group, the former students will likely all fail.

Grading systems that assume that all students can fit into a 30-point range are fine for homogeneous groups. When, however, you have readers mixed with nonreaders, students who perform well below grade level mixed with those who perform well above, and students with requisite knowledge mixed with those who lack it, it is impossible to create a single standard appropriate for all. Less than most groups, students in the typical ESL class will not fit into the 70- to 100% range.

INDIVIDUALIZED EDUCATION PLANS

If your classes are small, one possibility is to work from individual education programs (IEPs), as do special education teachers. With IEPs you can tailor the curriculum for students who have not attended much school. Such students can work with the main group when working on oral language, and work individually with you or an assistant when working on written material. Students who are identified as special education students will have IEPs (see Chapter 14) and you will have assistance in teaching them from the special education department.

If your classes are large and you have no assistants, the IEP option is not viable (except for special education students). Any special education teacher will tell you that simply creating and maintaining IEPs is time consuming, and much of the time consumed will be taken away from instruction. In addition, those teachers with large classes and no helpers will be able to give little individual attention to students working on individual curricula, thus defeating the purpose of the IEP in the first place. When 20 IEP students are working with one teacher, the teacher can do little more than hand everyone a different worksheet and hope for the best.

The worst option is to lower the standard to the point that everyone, even the students who have attended little school, can earn a 70 on daily work and tests. This option is exercised more than educators care to admit. If you teach to the least common denominator, you will not get any negative feedback for giving low grades, but your students will not learn as much as they should. Again, the range of ability, background, and motivation in your class will probably be vast. If you teach your class well, chances are that by Halloween your most successful students will already know more English than your least successful students will know at the end of the school year. It will not do to cheat one end of the bell curve in order to justify passing grades for the other.

MULTITRACK GRADING: SAME CLASS, DIFFERENT GOALS

One option for such situations is to grade on at least two tracks. You can call one a college-prep or pre-international commerce track and the other a general track. If you have nonreaders, you can have a separate track that includes basic literacy skills. In such a system, students in the top track would be graded strictly by the book with an emphasis on mastery of academic material. Those who cannot yet read any language would not have spelling grades included. Those who can read and write somewhat but are otherwise weak academically could be given extra credit for mastery of nonacademic, basic interpersonal communication skills (BICS). Such students will likely be in ESL longer than their better-prepared peers.

Even if you have some nonreaders, the class can still do many oral language activities together. If you have an assistant, volunteer help, computers, or language laboratory equipment, you will have the means to work on separate tracks. If not, do the best you can, but fight as hard as you can to get the equipment you need. If you are teaching students with third-grade skills alongside those with tenth-grade skills, you deserve the appropriate tools.

Even if you are not able to track within your class, all is not lost. Another option is to grade by the book, academics only, until grades drop below a certain point, let's say 85. Tell the students and their parents that grades above 85 reflect the demands of the academic track. When scores drop below 85, allow extra credit for nonacademic performance, or weigh oral language more heavily than written in grading those with weak writing skills.

Yet another option is to grade by skills mastered. You could determine that for the vocabulary part of the grade, the mastery of 200 vocabulary words in a six-week grading period merits a 70, and each 10 words or so beyond that minimum merit an extra point, up to the maximum of 100 points.

NO, YOU AREN'T CHEATING: WHAT COUNTS FOR GENERAL LEARNERS AND COLLEGE-PREP LEARNERS

It will not be dishonest of you to grade on a multitrack system. Again, unless you are one of the few ESL teachers working with homogeneous groups, you will be teaching different levels within your class. It is not unreasonable that you grade accordingly, as long as everyone understands what the grades mean.

Multitrack grading will not cause as much concern in an ESL class as it might in a college-prep class. One of the perks of teaching ESL is that students and their parents want mastery of the subject, and you can convince most of them that mastery matters more than the grades. While students in a college-prep class might be fighting for every fraction of a grade point they can get, your students and their parents know that an academic future in the United States begins with mastery of English, and everything else is of lesser significance. If a parent wants to know why her bright, hard-working son scored a 75 while the neighbor's child, who cannot yet read, scored a 78, explain that the former is being graded as a student who is expected to enter an all-English college-prep track within two or three years, while the neighbor's child is being graded on progress toward functional literacy and will probably remain in ESL for a longer period of time. Same class, different goals, and hence different standards.

TESTING, TESTING

Your students are going to get more than their share of testing. They will be tested before they enter your program and they will be tested at least once per year to determine if they are ready to exit from or change placement within the program. Depending on your state and the number of years they have studied in the United States, they may also take a standardized state test, and they will have the tests you give them.

You will give tests for two reasons. One, of course, is to determine what your students know. There is an expression in Spanish, *En el ojo del amo, engorda el gallo,* or the rooster seems to fatten in the eye of its owner. When we are involved in instruction, it can be easy to delude ourselves into believing that our students have progressed farther than they really have. If this causes us to allow our students to bypass essential skills, our students lose. Testing keeps our feet on the ground. Testing also lets the students and their parents know how much progress has been made.

Keeping Noses to the Grindstone

Tests are useful to keep students motivated. Most of us who attended college in the 1960s and 1970s took a class or two taught by forward-thinking professors who allowed us to grade ourselves. A few of our peers loved learning so much that they studied what they should have, but most of us took advantage of our professors' kindness and took it easy, so self-grading classes went the way of the dinosaur. Whether we like it or not, testing is a way to keep our students on their toes.

Testing Vocabulary

When testing vocabulary, translation is fast and efficient. You can dictate the word, use it in a sentence, and have the students write both the word in English and its meaning in their native language. This method does have certain disadvantages. Some would argue that any translation activity, at least for beginners, deters learners from thinking in English. This can sometimes be the case when too much translation and too little authentic language use goes on. If, however, students hear and use the vocabulary words many times in classroom activities, translating on test day will not do them any harm. If, however, your students speak a variety of languages or you cannot read your students' home language, this option is not viable.

When testing concrete vocabulary, you can test with pictures. You can provide answer sheets on which three drawings are offered as answer choices for each item. After you say a word or a sentence, have the students mark the correct picture. Or you can provide a copy of a photo or a drawing that includes a number of items and activities with answer blanks or identifying numbers or letters next to them. As you dictate words in English, your students can write them in the appropriate blanks.

You can also test vocabulary with multiple choice or true-or-false questions. You can ask beginning students if a cat is an animal, if your blouse is blue, if you are touching your nose, or if it is raining outside. Or you can ask, "Which of the following is a person? A. a cat; B. a boy; C. a house; or D. a car," or "Which item is cold? A. fire; B. the sun; C. an ice cube; D. a stove."

Some computer programs test vocabulary for you. Programs like *The Rosetta Stone* allow students to hear words and sentences and then ask them to click on a picture. Networked versions of some of these programs automatically log test results.

Testing Spelling

You can kill two birds with one stone by testing spelling and vocabulary together. If you provide quite a bit of exposure to vocabulary, you should find that most of your students can learn to recognize a lot of words each week. In my experience, most students can learn to at least understand 100 words per week if they have had ample exposure and opportunity to practice them. You will probably find that many of your students have a more difficult time spelling them all. You might want to designate some words as both spelling and vocabulary words and others as vocabulary words only. You can offer extra credit to those students who go the extra mile and learn to spell all the words that are on the vocabulary-only list.

The weekly spelling test is a good way to motivate your students to study their words. Spelling, however, is more than writing words in isolation. Grade spelling in dictation and authentic writing as well, but do not hold students responsible for spelling words that they have not yet studied.

Testing Speaking and Listening

Again, language consists of listening, speaking, reading, and writing. Because it is easiest to test reading and writing, sometimes listening and speaking skills are poorly monitored. Listening skills for beginners can be monitored with tests in which students hear a word, phrase, or sentence and respond by marking a picture or written word on a test sheet. Or you can give oral true-or-false tests or oral multiple choice tests in which you provide single-word answer choices. When students become more advanced, you can sometimes give tests in which you ask the question orally but require students to answer with complete written sentences.

Teachers can test speaking skills through controlled conversation, in which they ask select questions and note when the students can answer with the correct vocabulary and structure. Also useful are oral essay tests in which students respond to a question and the teacher notes which structures are attempted and which are used correctly. Or the teacher can keep a checklist for each student and note when skills are mastered based on observations of regular language use in the classroom.

Testing Grammar

If an examination does not test that which contributes to communication, it has little value. I could teach beginning English learners that the present participle ends in the suffix *ing* and then tell them to seek and identify such words in a test. Most students would then pass the test, erring only with a few confusing words like *thing* and *earring*. Or I could teach beginning Spanish learners that most words that end in *iera* or *ara* without an accent mark are verbs in the past subjunctive and then present a list of verbs and ask students to choose verbs in that tense. Those who learned my simple rule could answer my questions correctly, but that knowledge would have no value. For students who do not understand the past subjunctive or know how to apply it to produce useful sentences, such knowledge is useless trivia.

The best grammar tests are those that tell you if your students can apply the rules. Cloze tests like the one below work well for this purpose. Provide a sentence that is missing a key word, as in the following sentences.

Where _____ your sister live? She _____ in Dallas.
_____ you French? No, I _____ not. I am German.
_____ it rain tomorrow? No, I _____ think so.

Substitution activities also can be used to test active grammar skills. You can provide a paragraph like the following:

Tomorrow our class will go on a field trip. We will come to school at eight o'clock like we usually do. At nine o'clock we will get on a bus and go to a museum. We will eat a sack lunch at a picnic area behind the museum, and then we will go to a nearby art gallery. We will see paintings by some well-known local artists. At two o'clock, our teacher will take us back to the bus, and then we will come back to school. We will write an essay about our trip.

Have the students substitute the word *yesterday* for *tomorrow*, and then make all other appropriate changes in the passage. You can also provide passages with a singular subject, substitute a plural one, and have students make appropriate changes, or you can insert *don't* or *not* and require the students to change all verbs in the passage from affirmative to negative.

You can also test your students' active knowledge of grammar with questions that require them to answer in complete, grammatical sentences. *Where is your book? It is in my desk. Where did you live last year? I lived in Bolivia. What would you do if you heard the fire alarm? I would leave the building.*

SELF ASSESSMENT: GIVING STUDENTS THEIR OWN CHECKLISTS

It is important for students to monitor their own progress because it is impossible for us to peer inside our students' heads and see all that is going on there. You can create a checklist of language milestones and have your students note the date when each is met. The list can include but should not be limited to the following:

I understood a greeting.

I greeted someone in English and was understood.

I can name ten colors.

I can name ten articles of clothing.

I successfully ordered an item in a store or a restaurant.

I asked directions and understood the answer.

I gave directions.

I can sing an English song [name the song].

I understood an English song [name the song].

I told a joke in English and was understood.

I understood an English joke.

I had a conversation with an English speaker.

I understood part of the television news.

I understood part of the teacher's lecture in _____ class.

I understood most of the teacher's lecture in _____ class.

I can make statements in the present tense.

I can ask questions in the past tense.

I can tell about imaginary situations using *would*.

I watched an English-language movie and was able to follow the plot.

When all items on the list are checked, provide a new list with more demanding skills. When a student is feeling frustrated, produce the list and say, "Look how far you've come. Last January you couldn't even _____ and now you can _____, _____, and_____. " If a student tells a white lie on the self-assessment, use the lie as a motivational tool. "It says here that you can ask questions in the past tense, so why did you ask me, 'Where you go yesterday?'" At this point, a quick review of the use of the auxiliary verb *did* will likely be well received.

PREPARING STUDENTS FOR STANDARDIZED TESTS (PLEASE DON'T)

The trend toward including English learners in state assessments will result in better language learning even though, given the difficulty of learning a new language, it is not reasonable to expect them to perform on the same level as native speakers until they have had years of English study. It is, however, a great relief to no longer hear, "Who cares? They don't take the state test anyway." One negative side effect of this inclusion, however, is the tendency to teach to standardized tests, sometimes from the very beginning. It is essential that we do not put the cart before the horse. It is good to be able to use a semicolon correctly, but this is not a priority for someone who cannot yet orally produce a grammatical sentence.

Some teachers and administrators attempt to speed up their students' progress on paper by bypassing oral language and jumping right to the skills that are to be tested on written standardized tests. This never works. After students develop good listening skills, all contact with oral English becomes an English lesson. They learn new words in context, and grammatical structures are reinforced. Those who bypass this process miss out on a lot of language. Even if a narrow focus on items to be tested helps ratchet up test scores a few points in the short term, in the long term all academic indicators, including test scores, will suffer. It is unwise to attempt to teach language in a vacuum.

Working With Younger Students

Many young children learn oral language quickly and have fun doing it. It is part of your job to test and give grades, but be careful to not let the grading process crush a child's enthusiasm for language learning. The oral tests with picture answers are especially appropriate for young children who are learning oral English.

When making placement decisions for young children based on tests, keep in mind that sometimes test scores are more indications of what a child wants to tell you than of what the child really knows. When making such decisions for young children, it is important to also include information gleaned from observation.

14

Teaching English Learners With Special Needs

O ne of the most challenging aspects of ESL is teaching a foreign language, a truly demanding academic subject, to students who represent both ends and the middle of the bell curve. Yes, there are truly bilingual students with IQs in the 60s. As you might expect, such students exhibit delayed language development in both languages, their progress is much slower than that of their peers, and they struggle with reading and writing, but they learn to communicate effectively in two languages. Many become truly balanced bilinguals who handle one language as well as the other. Some English learners who experience only mild learning disabilities overcome or learn to compensate for them and go on to master English and succeed in their academic studies.

There was a time when schools that lacked programs for English learners placed recent immigrants in special education classes, not to meet their educational needs but to keep them away from the general population. I know people who immigrated to the United States in the 1940s and 1950s who spent their first few years in American schools copying, cutting, pasting, and coloring alongside mentally challenged native speakers of English simply because they could not speak the language of their teachers. This practice appears to be much rarer now than in the past.

It is a common misconception that in this day and age all minorities are overrepresented in special education. While it is true that the overall percentage of minority students enrolled in special education is slightly higher than that of the general population, the percentage of Hispanics and Asians, the two groups most likely to be served in bilingual or ESL programs, is not. According to the National Research Council Panel Report entitled "Minority Students in Special and Gifted Education," 11% of Hispanic students and 5% of Asian students are placed in special education, as opposed to 12% of non-Hispanic white students. Having politically correct numbers, however, does not mean that all is well.

IDENTIFYING STUDENTS WITH SPECIAL NEEDS

As with ESL, effective special education begins with appropriate placement. Whether, when, and how to place students in special education classes are indeed important and difficult questions. There are those who feel that one label is enough, and that, because students receive specialized instruction through their bilingual or ESL programs, placement in special education would be redundant. In a perfect world where funding and teachers' knowledge were without limit, this might be true. In the real world, we face limitations. Sooner or later you will have students who will benefit from special education teachers' expertise and the special education department's resources.

Before being placed in special education, most students will be tested by a psychologist or an educational diagnostician. Unlike the students in ESL or bilingual classes, special education students cannot be placed based on teacher-given tests. Students who do not speak English must be tested in their native language. Those who are bilingual but weak in English must be tested in both languages. The student must then qualify in both languages in order to receive special education services. If your district has no diagnostician who speaks the student's language, one must be contracted. This is expensive and inconvenient, so do not refer English learners frivolously. If a student is having problems in the first few months, take a wait-and-see attitude, unless it appears that there is a severe handicap. When it becomes clear that a student is having problems beyond those related to language learning, and you feel that he or she could benefit from special services, consider making a referral. Before doing so, however, you need to consider some special circumstances.

PRIOR EDUCATION, SEMILINGUALISM, AND LEARNING DISABILITIES

Students who are severely mentally challenged will be easy to identify, whatever the language issues. They can be identified with nonverbal tests or through observation in self-care situations. Those with learning disabilities, however, are another matter. This matter is complicated by the definitions of *learning disability*. The 2002 edition of *Wrightslaw: Special Education Law* states: "If a child has a disability that adversely affects educational performance . . . and is not negatively affected by environmental, cultural, or economic disadvantages, the child has a learning disability" (p. 30). Your students clearly are not disadvantaged by their culture, but there are some environmental and linguistic factors that might create the false impression that a student is learning disabled.

The exact legal definition of learning disability varies from state to state. At the time of this writing, in many states students are considered to be learning disabled if a significant discrepancy exists between IQ and academic performance.

Two issues must be considered when deciding whether a student who is struggling to learn English has a learning disability. First, some of your students may not have attended as much school as their classmates. Because many schools place immigrant students according to age rather than previous educational achievement, the sixteen-year-old who seems to be learning disabled may have attended only elementary school. Be certain that you know the student's level of prior schooling before making a special education referral. This is not to say that it is impossible for such students to be learning disabled, but if their skills are appropriate for the amount of schooling they have received, they probably are not. Your school, one hopes, will have resources to provide extra help for students who lack years of education in their native land.

A student who is semilingual may falsely appear to be learning disabled. Semilingualism occurs when a language learner speaks two languages but with a limited command of both. Few people are semilingual for a lifetime. Most either become dominant in one language or else eventually learn both well. It is not uncommon, however, for young people to experience a period of semilingualism while they are immersed and educated in a new language. A Spanish-speaking five-year-old in an English-language kindergarten might know the colors as *rojo, blue, verde* and *gray*. An older child might be more familiar with household and church-related vocabulary in Spanish but know scientific vocabulary only in English, the language of the textbooks. Some students who understand oral Spanish better than English read English better than Spanish. This is not a serious problem, just a temporary speed bump on the road to full mastery of English. Students tested while in this transitional state, however, will likely score lower in both English and in their home language than would students of similar ability who employ only one language.

If you speak the students' language, you may be able to identify such students. If a student can read and easily comprehend grade-level material in English as long as someone translates difficult vocabulary, chances are the supposed learning disability is a language matter. Good special education teachers keep their eyes open for signs that their students are on track to return to regular education. This is especially important for those who may have entered special education classes while still in a semi-lingual period.

WHAT DOES SPECIAL EDUCATION OFFER YOUR STUDENTS?

Some students, of course, will be best served by a combination of your services and those of the special education department. In a perfect world, schools with English learners would have at least one special education teacher who is knowledgeable in matters of language learning and at least one ESL teacher who is knowledgeable about special needs. If there are such people on your campus, or if you are such a person, your school is blessed. Unfortunately, both ESL/bilingual and special education teachers are currently in short supply, and dually trained teachers are even more rare. Nevertheless, you and the special education teachers can put your heads together and find ways to help the special students who need you both.

Before referring one of your students to special education, evaluate what special education will do and how you and the special education teachers can work together. Chances are you can work out a program that will benefit your English learner with special needs. Still, before making a referral, satisfy yourself that your student will benefit from the special services your school can offer. Remember that most special services are really "instead," not "extra." Time spent in special education is time not spent in your class (except in the case of inclusion), so decide whether the substitution is worthwhile.

WHEN THEY NEED A SPECIAL EDUCATION REFERRAL BUT HAVEN'T GOTTEN ONE

It is important to note that students who would benefit from or have great need for special education services sometimes get locked out. Sometimes teachers and administrators are too reluctant to refer English learners to special education. Even on the Texas-Mexico border where I live, even in schools with populations that are almost entirely Hispanic, some bilingual teachers complain that they meet with more resistance than do teachers of all-English language classes when they refer students to special education.

I once worked in a mostly Hispanic middle school where the special education population was disproportionately non-Hispanic. That year, probably a full third of my ESL students were English dominant, and a few barely spoke Spanish at all. Some of them had entered kindergarten speaking only Spanish but had mastered English in the ensuing eight years. Because they continued to be weak academically, they were never exited from ESL classes. Others had been English dominant their entire lives but were placed in ESL based on poor academic performance. One student's mother told me that she had been persuaded to falsely declare on the home language survey that her family spoke principally Spanish at home. She had been told that this was the only way for her son to get the help he needed to avoid failing.

Many of these students would have been better served in special education, but attempts to refer them met with endless bureaucratic roadblocks. The administration's philosophy was that students with vowels at the end of their names probably just needed more English, and, year after year, English-dominant but possibly learning-disabled students were placed with recent immigrants.

This philosophy, of course, created disappointing results. Placing learning disabled children in classes designed for English learners is as unethical and harmful as placing English learners in classes meant to serve the learning disabled and mentally challenged. Dealing with a learning disability by reviewing the rudiments of one's native language is like treating diabetes with chemotherapy.

DETERMINING THE APPROPRIATE PROGRAM

After testing the student, a diagnostician or psychologist will determine if he or she qualifies for special education services. Once a student qualifies, a committee consisting of the child's parent(s) and school personnel will determine placement. The committee will also write or approve an individual education program. In most states, this is called an IEP (individual education program) committee, although we Texans call it the ARD (admission, review, dismissal) committee. Depending on your state's rules and whether the student has other teachers, you may or may not be required to participate in this process. Even if you are not required to participate, your student will likely benefit if you do so.

Schools are required to provide a variety of services to students with special needs. Those with only mild learning disabilities might spend all of their class time in regular classes with very little intervention from special education personnel. Others might be served by inclusion teachers. These are itinerant special education teachers who serve mainstreamed students in their regular classrooms. Students might divide their academic day between your classroom and a special education classroom, or they might go to the special education room only when they need extra help. Severely handicapped students might spend the entire school day in a special classroom, in which case you might be the itinerant teacher who comes in to assist. The IEP committee has a great deal of power. Whatever the IEP committee determines, within the limits of the law of course, must be followed.

If the IEP committee so determines, you can offer slower paced instruction, a different kind of instruction, shortened assignments, modified grading, or extra help from special education teachers. In many school districts special education is better funded than is ESL. If there is material or equipment that a dually labeled student needs, it might be easier to fund through special education.

If a student is having difficulty with oral language, the IEP committee may specify an extra dose. You might want to have a student practice oral English in the special education classroom while your other students do more advanced written work, and then move the special student into written English later on, perhaps even in a later year. Controlled conversation (described in Chapter 10) is a good technique when there are small groups of English learners in a special education class or when the special education teacher can give the student one-on-one attention. For severely challenged students, a heavy dose of TPR (Total Physical Response) with a lot of repetition may be appropriate. This technique has proven effective even with nonverbal students.

If you are teaching a bilingual class that includes reading in the native language, the IEP committee will determine which language to use in the special education classroom. If the student is doing fairly well in oral English but is reading badly in both languages, the committee might choose to continue native-language reading in the special education classroom until a basic level of literacy is attained. On the other hand, if the student has fair English literacy skills, or if the student has a fair mastery of oral English but few reading skills in any language, the committee might decide to teach only English reading in the special education classroom.

Working With Younger Students

The majority of students who are placed in special education are identified as learning disabled. It is very difficult to identify K–2 students in this way. The learning disabled label is based on a difference between perceived intelligence and academic skills, and it is difficult to establish the existence of a learning ability for those who have been studying academic skills for so such a short time. The Individuals with Disabilities Education Act (IDEA) does, however, allow that young children can qualify for special education based on developmental delay.

15

English Learners in Content Classes

Depending on student age, state rules, school policies, and the decisions of placement committees, beginning English learners may begin studying math, social studies, and science in the English language from their first day in school. English learners may be taught content in special sheltered English classes, taught by either ESL teachers (if state laws permit) or teachers who specialize in the subject taught, or they may be placed in regular content classes, with or without support from the ESL department. Each approach has its appropriate applications.

ENGLISH THROUGHOUT THE CURRICULUM

There is a saying in Spanish, *quien mucho abarca, poco aprieta,* or he who grasps much, holds little. Some ESL programs set ambitious goals that are never met. To fully master a language in a few years is a major task, even without having to study other subjects. To master a language while learning all other required subjects as well is even more so. To do so is a little like maintaining an A average in school while participating in half a dozen extracurricular activities. Such an accomplishment is possible, but not for all students. At least during the first year or two of study, you will be justified in stressing mastery of English, even if said mastery comes at the expense of other academics.

SHELTERED ENGLISH CONTENT CLASSES

Sheltered English instruction—also known as content ESL, English for specific purposes (ESP), content based instruction (CBI), and specially designed academic instruction in English (SDAIE)—allows English learners to study these subjects in segregated classes with special books and materials. In sheltered English classes for absolute beginners, it might be a good idea to spend the first few months working on related vocabulary using realia, pictures, and such techniques as Total Physical Response (TPR). Once students approach an intermediate command of English, they may study these subjects much as they would in regular classes, except that the teacher will control vocabulary when speaking and the textbooks will contain simpler vocabulary and structures. In sheltered English classes, beginning students will likely learn less of the subject than they would if they were studying in their native language, but they will learn more English.

CONTENT OBJECTIVES AND LANGUAGE OBJECTIVES

Again, to learn a language is no small matter. One will not master a new language in a few years by studying it only an hour or two per day. If your students are required to take all academic subjects, there will be only an hour or two left per day to specifically study English. The good news is that the content classes can also be vehicles for the instruction of English. When students reach a solid intermediate level and are able to understand much of what they hear, immersion in English may become the best lesson of all. At this point, they should be able to divine the meaning of many new expressions from the context, and they should be able to direct their own English learning with tools like bilingual dictionaries.

For less advanced students, you will want to teach all subjects with language objectives in mind. Lesson plans for sheltered science, social studies, and math classes for beginning and intermediate language learners should include both language and content objectives.

Extremely broad language objectives, such as "The learner will speak in complete sentences," or "Students will use sophisticated vocabulary," or "Learners will pronounce correctly" are too wide and vague to provide much guidance, and are really no better than no language objective at all. Narrower language objectives can, however, be extremely useful. Because vocabulary is key to both language learning and mastery of core subjects, the sheltered English approach is especially appropriate for vocabulary development.

A SAMPLE SHELTERED SCIENCE/VOCABULARY LESSON

A teacher in a sheltered English class can use many of the techniques described in the previous chapters either to teach new content or to use content to teach English. It is reasonable that much of the science taught to English learners be of the hands-on variety. In such a situation, you can mix science instruction with TPR. A lesson like the one that follows would be appropriate even for students who have had only a month or two of English instruction. The classic baking-soda-and-vinegar science experiment can demonstrate the nature of chemical reactions and teach a dozen new vocabulary words at the same time.

Begin by dividing the class into groups. Provide each group with a test tube, a beaker, a flask, a teaspoon, a tablespoon, and a balloon. Say, "Pick up a test tube. No, Pedro, that's a beaker. Juan has a test tube. Juan, hold up a test tube. Everybody look at Juan. That's a test tube." You could say *probeta*, but in this case, a translation would be unnecessary and would get in the way of your students' thinking in English.

Now, hold up a bottle of vinegar and say, "I have a bottle of vinegar that I am going to pass around. Pour about 15 milliliters into your test tube." Hold up a graduated cylinder and pour in some vinegar. Write "15" on the board if your students are still struggling with numbers. Then pour the vinegar into your test tube. Distribute the vinegar to the groups of students. Say, "Now we will pour a few milliliters of oil into the test tube to separate the baking soda from the vinegar." Produce cooking oil in its original container (so that students will recognize it) and pour some on top of the vinegar. Say, "The oil will separate the vinegar and the soda to prevent a chemical reaction until we are ready to produce one. Now gently pour the oil on top of the vinegar." Demonstrate the action.

Say, "You have a teaspoon and a tablespoon in front of you [demonstrate both]. Pick up the teaspoon. No, Hideo, that's the tablespoon. Pick up the teaspoon [demonstrate again]. Take the box of baking soda [hold up a box of baking soda]. Now measure out one half teaspoon of baking soda." Write "1/2" on the board. If a student puts too much or too little baking soda on the spoon, point to the fraction on the board, and demonstrate. Say to the student who made a mistake, "No, Horst, you measured out a full teaspoon. I want half a teaspoon." Point to the fraction on the board again and show the class a teaspoon that is half full.

Now say, "Gently sprinkle the soda into the test tube" as you demonstrate the action. "Be careful to *not* shake the test tube yet." Early in the course, you can demonstrate negativity by shaking your head as you demonstrate an action. If you shake your head as you shake an empty test tube, your students will understand your meaning. Next, tell them to pick up the balloon. If your students are still learning colors and shapes, you can quickly review by asking who has a red balloon, who has a green one, who has a round one, and who has a long one.

Point to the mouth of the test tube and say, "This is the mouth of the test tube." If they know the more common meaning of the word, you can alternately point to your own mouth and the mouth of the test tube and say, "This is a mouth, and so is this." Place the balloon over the mouth of the test tube. "Now shake the test tube. [Demonstrate both actions.] When the baking soda mixes with the vinegar, it creates a chemical reaction that produces carbon dioxide." Spanish speakers may recognize the cognates for *reacción química* and *dióxido de carbon* if you speak slowly and clearly and emphasize the words *chemical reaction* and *carbon dioxide*. Say, "The reaction will make your balloons inflate." Demonstrate inflation with gestures. "Look, Juan's balloon is inflating. So is Chloe's. Which balloon has inflated the most? Which has inflated the least? Whose balloon did not inflate?"

In this lesson you will have taught the words and phrases *vinegar, oil, test tube, baking soda, balloon, milliliter, half, teaspoon, shake,* and *inflate* in a hands-on fashion, and you will have reviewed and exposed your students to several others. If your vocabulary goal for your students is 100 new vocabulary words per week in all classes combined, you will have covered half of the day's vocabulary requirement in a 30-minute science experiment, and you will have demonstrated a scientific principle as well.

USING SHELTERED ENGLISH TO TEACH AND PRACTICE GRAMMAR

After you introduce grammatical structures, either explicitly or implicitly through modeling or pattern practice in ESL class, you can reinforce use of that structure in a sheltered content class. In a history class for advanced beginners, use of the past tense is an appropriate language objective. After all, history is about the past. Early in the course, the language objective might be the correct use of the past forms of the linking verbs *was* and *were*. *Lincoln was the sixteenth president of the United States. Mexico was part of New Spain. Louis XVI and Marie Antoinette were French monarchs.* Later in the courses, you could add statements in the past tense with regular and common irregular verbs. *The Greeks had a democratic form of government. Columbus discovered American and claimed it for Spain. Hitler's army invaded Poland.* Later still you could add the past of less common irregular verbs as well. At different times in the social studies course, you can include negative statements in the past and later questions in the past.

When discussing the day's news after reading the newspaper or watching a television newscast, the language objective could be the use of the present progressive. *Rain is falling in Mississippi. The Fredonian army is advancing on Oceana. People in Canada are voting today.*

In a lesson in which students are called on to speculate about future events, the language objective could be the correct use of the words *will* and *might*. *The Olympics will take place next year*, or *Leaders of Pacifica might call for independence.*

For more advanced English learners, the language objective of a social studies class might be the use of complex sentences to explain cause and effect. *It will snow in the Northeast because a cold front is coming in from Canada*, or *A lot of people will be unemployed in Townsville because the tire plant will close next month.*

Choosing Appropriate Materials for Sheltered English Classes

With sheltered English you will have the advantage of being able to choose appropriate materials for your students. Although the vocabulary in the regular textbooks is important, to teach grade-level English vocabulary to students who know only a few thousand words is definitely putting the cart before the horse, unless, of course, those words are cognates for words in their native language.

Avoid the temptation to select regular grade-level textbooks and then modify by translating everything into the students' native language. If you are going to teach a subject almost entirely in another language, you should have books in that language. To help students limp through material they cannot understand with constant translation cheats them out of both English and content. It is good to have material that challenges the students; if the book is too difficult for the students to understand without constant intervention from the teacher, however, get a different book.

When choosing books for your sheltered English students, consider both age and language ability. Do not give high school students who read at a third-grade level books written for eight-year-olds. Secondary students' background knowledge is greater than that of those in elementary school. There are a great many textbooks on the market specifically written for English learners. Take advantage of them.

WHEN ARE STUDENTS READY TO WADE INTO THE MAINSTREAM?

Sooner or later English learners will need to enter the academic mainstream. The questions of when and how long are difficult ones and will vary from student to student. Again, sink-or-swim immersion is folly, but stay-out-of–the-water-until-you-know-how-to-swim segregation is worse. We must have high expectations for English learners, and we need to keep them in contact with native speakers, but it does no good to simply drop non-English speakers into regular classes and demand the impossible.

When Are Students Ready for the Mainstream?

It is a good idea to allow students to take nonacademic classes with native speakers from their first day in school. Art and physical education classes are good places to mix with native speakers. If possible, English learners in these classes should not be seated next to other English learners. After the first semester, some students will be ready for regular math classes if tutoring support is available. An elite few might be ready for other academic classes as well. This transfer of students will reduce the number of students in your class and allow you to provide more intensive instruction for students who made less-than-adequate progress in the first semester. In the second year, you or the placement committee can decide which students are ready for one, two, or three mainstream academic classes.

Regular education teachers too often have English learners dropped into their classrooms without any guidelines for what should be expected of them. It is not enough to place students in the mainstream and give teachers orders to motivate, modify, and give passing grades. Too often, frustrated teachers of students who were mainstreamed prematurely end up encouraging their charges to simulate learning by writing something — anything, even a word-for-word reproduction of the question—in the blanks of their worksheets and tests. The message becomes, "Look busy, put something on paper, and take your C." Unfortunately, some students who learn to get by in this manner may limp through several years of school without learning study skills, or much of anything else. Your students need not understand everything that they hear and read in regular content classes to benefit, but they must have some clues.

A very few students, the very quickest learners, will be ready to succeed in the mainstream after as little as a semester. In the higher grades these will be students who have strong academic skills in their native languages and who are willing to spend several extra hours studying with the aid of bilingual dictionaries. Most, however, will need some modifications during the first few years. The modifications must be more than simply passing them because they do not speak English.

THE POWER OF PRIOR KNOWLEDGE

Clearly the task is more difficult when the student is new to the content. If a Spanish speaker understands that *células* have *núcleos* with *cromosomas* inside, a lesson on cellular biology can be a useful English lesson, even if the student learns nothing new about biology. If students are familiar with the countries of Europe, they can learn their English names easily when the teacher points to them on a map and says their names. For students who know nothing of these countries, the task is more difficult. It is clearly easier to learn a new label for something than to come to understand its nature. When considering whether to place students in a sheltered English class or in the mainstream, consider their prior knowledge of the subject.

THE POWER OF INCIDENTAL LEARNING

When deciding whether to place a student in a regular class, consider the value of incidental learning there. Often students who appear to flounder in the mainstream, even some who receive failing grades there, learn a lot of language. Sometimes students who get complacent in the sheltering arms of sheltered English classes need the reality therapy that a period or two of true English immersion offers.

In this age of accountability, we teachers are expected to express our instructional intent in lesson plans, teach the material, and then prove through some sort of assessment that the material has been mastered. The downside is that this "accountability" downplays the value of incidental learning, that which does not appear on the lesson plans. If an English teacher covering a Shakespeare lesson goes off on a tangent about British royal succession and children learn about three or four kings who were not listed in the lesson plans, or a math teacher who plays classical music in the background familiarizes his students with the works of Europe's best-known composers, valuable lessons are learned, even if the teacher does not get to take credit for that learning. It has been said that people can accomplish great things when they are not concerned about who will take credit. There is no simple way to evaluate incidental learning, but ethical teachers share it whenever they can.

Incidental learning is especially powerful in language learning situations. All contact with the English language is valuable for those who are learning it. Content class teachers who perpetually feel frustrated by the difficulties their students face might be surprised at the amount of language that English learners are picking up in their classes.

One does not learn vocabulary all at once. Mastery of vocabulary may begin when a student looks up a word in a dictionary, copies it from the blackboard, or sees it demonstrated by an ESL teacher, but it is not complete until the student has heard and used the word several times. The same holds true for grammatical structures. Even if one knows the rules of English grammar, it takes months or even years to learn to apply them correctly and automatically. The modeling of correct English structures that students encounter, among other places, in the content classroom contributes to ultimate mastery.

Students sometimes report learning a word that they seemingly had never heard and then hearing it five times later that day in their regular classes. Some students also report missing words on a vocabulary test in ESL class and then hearing and understanding them in another class an hour later. Teachers report meeting English learners who had been in their classes in past years and who seemed to learn nothing there but who had since become fluent and thank the teacher for helping make that fluency possible.

Students who seem to be learning nothing in the mainstream may be picking up vocabulary and reinforcing structure as they listen, even if they appear to understand very little. There is good reason for the frustrated classroom teacher to take heart.

REASONABLE AND UNREASONABLE MODIFICATIONS IN THE INCLUSIVE CLASSROOM

Before sending students into a regular content classroom, determine which modifications are reasonable. Mainstream teachers should allow English learners to use appropriate reference materials, including bilingual dictionaries, even on tests. If students understand the content but express their knowledge imperfectly because of language difficulties, those imperfections should be given little weight in grading. Teachers might even want to consider allowing first-year mainstreamed students to answer test questions in their native language when they know the answer but cannot express it in English. The English-learner label must not, however, become a license to pass simply for showing up.

THE F WORD (FAILURE)

Unfortunately, in many schools the first priority is to get the students through in the least possible amount of time. When a student comes to an American school in tenth grade with no English skills, or in seventh grade with neither English language skills nor native-language literacy skills, it is difficult to master the language and content skills necessary to graduate by the age of eighteen. The F word (failure) is unpopular, but sometimes retention or repetition of a course can be positive. It is better to repeat a year and graduate late or finish in night school for adults than to be held to no standard and be passed on year after year, and to graduate limited in both English language and academic skills. Given the difficult situation that English learners in regular classes face, it is reasonable that they be allowed to take these classes on an A–B–C / no credit basis.

THE BRIGHT SIDE: ENRICHED CLASS DISCUSSIONS

Many regular content-class teachers have happy tales about their experiences with English learners mainstreamed into their classes. Foreign students with different points of view can make class discussions interesting. Some English learners have levels of knowledge superior to that of their American-born classmates. I was once presenting background information for Charles Dickens's novel *A Tale of Two Cities* in an English literature class and I asked who knew about the storming of the Bastille. All five of the students who knew had attended school in Mexico. Some intermediate English learners have done better with Shakespeare than their native-English-speaking peers, perhaps because they have learned to not be frustrated by words and phrases they do not understand, or perhaps because learning English has helped them hone their skills at applying context clues.

OUT-OF-CLASS SUPPORT FOR ENGLISH LEARNERS IN REGULAR CONTENT CLASSES

ESL teachers can provide support for English learners in regular classes in a number of ways. You can offer tutoring services before or after school, or you can offer support during the regular academic day. If you have a long ESL block, you might set aside a half-hour per day for homework help or to help clarify that which is taught in the mainstream. Another option is to offer a daily homework help session in place of an elective. Administrators might complain that such a noncredit session is a waste of time. Remember the adage *To grasp at much is to hold little*. It is better to receive one fewer credit per year than to not understand that which is taught in content classes.

In tutoring situations, limited translation of key concepts is reasonable, even if the student is not enrolled in a bilingual program. If a student is going to spend two weeks working problems involving triangles, it is not unreasonable to spend ten minutes of tutoring time explaining the Pythagorean theory in the student's native language. For students who spend several hours daily fully immersed in English, a bit of translation will not interfere with progress toward mastery of English.

16

Helping Everyone Else Understand Your Students

ATTITUDES MAKE THE DIFFERENCE: RACISM AND XENOPHOBIA

The attitudes of the teachers and administrators are at least as important as those of the students. While racism and xenophobia are not as pervasive as some of the more radical education writers have suggested, they do exist and they can do a lot of damage to an ESL program. Klansmen will not be burning crosses at your classroom door, but some people in your school hierarchy may be making decisions that hinder your students' progress. For the most part, teachers and administrators want their students to succeed, but there are exceptions. I can recall a few teachers and administrators who actually became hostile when they saw recent arrivals becoming too successful.

Several years ago I applied for a position teaching ESL in a west Texas high school. It was midterm, and the class had been taught by an uncertified, nondegreed substitute for an entire semester. The principal told me that until recently they had managed to keep "those kids" in the city's other high school. The students were taught in a separate classroom, apart from the mainstream, but they had no ESL materials. I did not get the job, but neither did anyone else. The school finished the year with the substitute.

This is, of course, a worst-case scenario. In my 25 years of working with English learners, I have encountered serious bias against my students only three times, but my students have had their share of petty problems.

I'M HERE, SO SHUT THE DOOR ALREADY

When asked his thoughts as he took the oath of U.S. citizenship, Russian immigrant and comedian Yakov Smirnoff replied, "I was thinking about those damned foreigners who come here and take jobs away from us good Americans." This typifies the attitudes of many of us. We are proud of our immigrant roots, but we're here, so why hasn't somebody closed the door?

You cannot assume that attitude problems necessarily end when students deal with those of their own ethnic group. Minorities are individuals with their own view of the world, and not all hyphenated Americans are comfortable with recent arrivals. A huge cultural gap exists between a monolingual English-speaking Chinese-American and a recent arrival from Beijing, or between a fifth-generation Mexican-American from the suburbs of Dallas and a farm worker from Oaxaca, Mexico.

A few times each year someone suggests to me that we should not even be letting "those people" in the country, much less providing their children with a quality education. If you encounter such an attitude from a barfly, just let him rave. If you encounter it in someone who has any control over your program, do as much damage control as you can. If you encounter it in yourself, engage in some serious reflection.

You cannot change attitudes easily. You can explain reasons for immigration: It has brought vibrancy to our culture and prosperity to our economy, and it has helped us maintain peace on our borders. As our population ages, immigration brings us the workers that will sustain the economy as the baby boomers retire. If that doesn't work, try this: Remind detractors that a school can rot from the bottom up. Poor readers who see non-English speakers getting passing grades will demand the same. Literate but mediocre students will want B's because illiterates get C's. Adequate students then demand A's. When children learn English and go on to succeed in honors classes after three years or four years, there may be some resentment, but the effects of the competition that these successful students bring will benefit all students, and they will be part of a rising tide that lifts all boats. If English learners fail to learn year after year, that failure will become part of a rot at the base that will bring down the entire structure.

EXPOSING OTHER STUDENTS
TO YOUR STUDENTS' CULTURE

If students in regular classes are exposed to your students' culture(s), everyone will benefit. It is, however, important to not be heavy handed when presenting the culture of your students to the other students of your school. Remember that xenophobia does exist, and you do not want to create the impression that your school will be forcing elements of your students' culture on everyone else. It will be useful, however, to expose your school's students to your students' background through regular academic study.

AVOIDING TRIVIAL PURSUIT AND SUPERFICIAL MULTICULTURALISM

A young Dakota woman at my alma mater once ran out of a lecture hall in tears during a sociology professor's lecture about poverty and social problems on reservations like the one that the young woman called home. The professor thought he was expressing a politically correct viewpoint, but he came across as condescending. Chances are that none of your students will flee your class in tears, but a trivial treatment of their culture, even if the intention is to celebrate it or to express sympathy, may cause resentment.

It is important that you not trivialize your students' culture, but sometimes well-meaning educators do just that. Unfortunately, a lot of phony multiculturalism exists in our schools. Merely ordering take-out lunches from Taco Bell on the Fifth of May or wearing a silk robe for the Chinese New Year or a pair of *lederhosen* during *Fasching* will neither educate nor inspire. Although there is nothing wrong with eating ethnic food or wearing national or regional clothing, your lessons should be based on knowledge, not just gimmicks.

Knowledge is the key that will allow you to enlighten rather than trivialize. If you lack requisite knowledge, use the knowledge of the great minds of the past. Literature is a great window to the culture. American anthropologist Ruth Benedict, who wrote *The Chrysanthemum and the Sword*: *Patterns of Japanese Culture*, had never visited Japan. To do so would have been difficult, since she wrote the book during World War II at the request of the Bureau of Overseas Intelligence of the Office of War. Her book was so accurate that some scholars in Japan insisted that it was really written by a Japanese turncoat. Benedict's knowledge of Japan was based in great part on what she had learned by reading history and literature.

ILLUMINATING WITH LITERARY CLASSICS FROM OTHER TRADITIONS

When I told a group of my acquaintances that I was taking a Latin American literature class, one person commented, "I didn't think that they had literature. I thought they just made velvet paintings and wood carving." Clearly this fellow was not particularly enlightened, but his attitude and his shallow knowledge of the world beyond our borders is not uncommon.

All cultures with written languages have large bodies of literature, and you might want to work some of that literature into your school's English or reading curriculum. A great many Spanish-language works are universally held to be masterpieces. *Don Quijote* is the most influential book ever written in the Spanish language and is considered by scholars throughout the world to be among the most important works of fiction ever written. It is too large a work to be read in its entirety in a high school course, except perhaps in a very advanced honors class, but selections from a translation of the work could be taught in any high school literature class. An abridged version could be taught as well. The *Wishbone Classics* series has a version written on a fourth-grade level that catches the spirit of the work as well as any children's version I have ever seen. Miguel de Cervantes is also known for his Exemplary novels (which are really not novels but long short stories) and his hilarious short plays, any of which are well worth reading or viewing. Of course, Cevantes's era, referred to as the Golden Century, produced many other fine writers whose works are also worth studying.

Latin America has produced its share of great literature as well. *Pedro Paramo*, a short novel by the Mexican author Juan Rulfo, is arguably the best ghost story ever written and is steeped with Mexican culture and history. The Argentine author Jorge Borges produced some of the finest short stories of the twentieth century.

Advanced students in high school literature classes could read translations of novels of the Latin American Boom by writers like Gabriel Garcia Marques, Carlos Fuentes, and Mario Vargas Llosa. For younger readers, there are a great many collections of children's stories from many different cultures available.

LIVING SOCIAL STUDIES

The presence of your students can enhance your school's social studies programs. Again, you do not want to inflame feelings of xenophobia by creating the impression that you feel that your students' history is more important than that of our country, but the presence of students from other places justifies special emphasis within social studies classes. Your students' parents can be wonderful resources. Some of them might be willing to address geography and history classes. These subjects come alive when students meet people who have lived in the lands and experienced the events described in their books.

GRAPHIC ART AND MUSIC

Art, including folk art, from your students' home nations can be presented and studied in art classes. Some works of art like the murals of Diego

Rivera, Jose Clemente Orozco, and David Alfaro Siqueiros depict historical events and are therefore appropriate for history classes. Classical, folk, and even popular music can be worked into the music curriculum. Music can be played in the background in any classroom, and copies of paintings can hang on any wall. The teacher can speak a bit about roots and circumstances related to the works when the class has some free time.

MUTUAL TUTORING AND DUAL IMMERSION

If your school offers your students' language as a second language, some of your students who were tutored by student volunteers could return the favor by helping in foreign language classes or conversing at meetings of foreign language clubs. Mutual tutoring will not only help students understand each other's languages, it can also help them understand each other.

17

Preparing Yourself to Be a Better ESL Teacher

I f you find yourself in circumstances that force you to begin teaching ESL with less-than-adequate preparation, you will have plenty of opportunities to improve your knowledge of language and teaching. If you are teaching on an emergency permit or you hold certification based on only a few college classes or inservice sessions, you will certainly benefit from further academic study. Although it is important to continue your undergraduate or postgraduate education, you can also do a great deal beyond taking classes in linguistics and methodology.

CATCHING UP AND KEEPING UP WITH ADVANCES IN THE FIELD

Whether or not you take university classes in language teaching methodology, you should keep up with what is going on in the field. Be open to different methodologies, but be careful to not be seduced by them. Sometimes methodologies can be narrow, some may be inappropriate for your students, and a few are absolutely crackpot. Some methods are tied to certain schools of psychology or linguistics, and sometimes the scholars who promote them are more concerned with trying to make reality conform to their theories than with providing methods that work. Sometimes scholars get involved in intellectual turf wars. You have probably seen articles written by bilingual or ESL scholars that disparage what is being done by teachers of foreign languages, or vice versa. Do not be swayed by allegiances. Techniques used in bilingual or foreign language classes may work very well for you. Be especially wary of innovators whose methods require you to buy expensive materials that they happen to sell. Their work may be more salesmanship than scholarship. You are on the front lines, and you need methods that work.

Judge a method on its effectiveness, not its intellectual pedigree. If you encounter a new technique that seems promising, try it out, both on yourself and on your students. If it is a technique for absolute beginners, try it on yourself with a language you do not know. If it does not yield the results you expected, try something else. If you see that another teacher has had success with a technique that failed with you, find out what is different and try it again, with modifications. Remember, however, that one man's medicine is another's poison. A technique that is effective with one sort of students may be less effective with another. Also, some techniques may be better suited to your talents and style than others.

Read widely about the field. The books listed in Appendix 2 will get you started. Some books are eclectic, covering a number of sometimes contradictory theories and approaches. Such books may be confusing to new teachers, but it is worth the trouble to consider diverse points of views. Other books are narrower and easier to follow. Such books can be valuable, but read them with a critical eye.

A number of good periodicals deal with language teaching, some of which are listed in the appendix. The appendix also lists some Web sites for ESL teachers. These sites provide links to articles about language teaching and to providers of language teaching materials. Some also have chat rooms where you can communicate with other ESL teachers.

ACQUAINTING YOURSELF WITH YOUR STUDENTS' CULTURE

If your students' culture is not familiar to you, learn as much about it as you can. Get to know people in the community, and read widely. History and literature are great windows into other people's worlds. If you have students from Mexico, you will see something of them in the essays and poetry of Nobel Laureate Octavio Paz. While the revolutionary campesino soldiers of Mario Azuela's *The Underdogs* may no more resemble urban teenagers in your class than the revolutionary Minutemen resemble white teenagers in a suburb of Chicago, the hand of the past shapes us all.

TRYING ON YOUR STUDENTS' SHOES

Although it is important to learn about language acquisition, it is at least as important to experience it firsthand. No matter what techniques are used, language learning in the classroom cannot be exactly like learning one's native language. Unfortunately, many ESL teachers lack the experience of learning any language other than their primary one. Monolingual teachers and administrators who work with English learners will benefit if they learn another language. There is much about learning languages that is obvious to those who have had that experience but a total mystery to those who have not. Much of our judgment is based on introspection, and that introspection is based on our experience.

A command of languages also will give a teacher greater credibility in the eyes of students and their parents, as well as a certain moral authority. It is easier to make a good impression on your students' parents if you speak to them directly rather than through a translator. This is especially true when the teacher is bringing bad news. It is not so difficult to speak through a translator to tell parents that their child has earned a spot on the honor roll, but to report that a student is failing or will be suspended from school. . . . That is a different matter. When a student or a parent demands to know how you can ask your class to do demanding work in a new language, it helps to be able to respond, "I read *Don Quijote/Les Miserables/Crime and Punishment* in the language in which it was written. It was difficult, but worthwhile. I would recommend the experience to anyone."

As with the students, you will not attain nativelike fluency in a single year unless you have a nearly superhuman aptitude for language learning. Given that your students have more time to learn your language than you have to learn theirs, you can be forgiven if your progress is less than theirs. Nevertheless, your effort will be noted and respected.

Those who are at least bilingual can benefit by taking an occasional literature class taught in their other language. It would also be a good idea to dabble in a third, fourth, or fifth language, if only to keep in touch with the realities of language learning.

The more that a teacher knows a language, the better, but not all teachers will have time to attain near-native fluency. ESL teachers should strive to eventually at least reach a level at which they can follow conversations, read books, and communicate in writing in a second language. This may take a few years, but it will be worth the effort. Remember that your students must someday do academic work in their new language. You will be better prepared to help your students make this challenging step if you have had a similar experience yourself.

Those administrators who deal directly with language learners or those who teach beginning English learners in the mainstream might consider learning to become able to communicate at least at a basic level in a second language, if only to sensitize themselves to the situation their students face. If you can speak a second language, you might offer to teach the rudiments of it to them, for a reasonable fee of course.

Language learning, although arduous and often frustrating, can be exhilarating as well. Experiencing the joys that come with the mastery of a new language will make one a better language teacher. Besides, a commitment to learning a language gives an educator a good excuse to spend a summer or two, or even a sabbatical year, in a foreign country.

A summer trip to Europe, Asia, or nearby Mexico or Quebec accompanied by an intensive language course would be both entertaining and enlightening. A teacher who takes a one-year leave of absence to teach English and either formally or informally study a language abroad will certainly return better-prepared to teach English at home.

AND IF YOU TEACH IN THE TOWER OF BABEL . . .

Those teachers who have students who speak a variety of languages cannot, of course, be expected to learn the language of each. By learning at least one language, however, such a teacher will be more in tune with his or her students' situation and will command greater respect from students and their parents.

A study of comparative linguistics and a knowledge of the International Phonetics Alphabet will give such teachers the tools they need to adjust instruction according to the nature of the students' native languages. It is a good idea for teachers to know at least a little about the languages of all students in their classes, if only to know which sounds, structures, and concepts are likely to be difficult for them. Good bilingual dictionaries provide much of this information.

Good luck and God speed. May you be successful in helping children and young adults make their first steps into academic study in the English language. I sincerely hope that your experience working with English learners will be as rewarding as mine has been.

Appendix 1

Vocabulary Lists

Numbers 1–10

1 one _____

2 two _____

3 three _____

4 four _____

5 five _____

6 six _____

7 seven _____

8 eight _____

9 nine _____

10 ten _____

Shapes

a circle _____

a triangle _____

a square _____

a rectangle _____

a star _____

an oval _____

a cube _____

a pyramid _____

a sphere _____

a straight line _____

a curved line _____

an angle _____

Numbers 11–20

11 eleven _____

12 twelve _____

13 thirteen _____

14 fourteen _____

15 fifteen _____

16 sixteen _____

17 seventeen _____

18 eighteen _____

19 nineteen _____

20 twenty _____

People and Things

a girl _____

a boy _____

a baby _____

a man _____

a woman _____

a watch _____

a fan _____

a book _____

a ring _____

a key _____

a person _____

people _____

a thing _____

things _____

Note to the teacher: After students learn to identify people and objects, have them classify specific nouns as people or things.

Numbers by Tens to 100

ten _____

twenty _____

thirty _____

forty _____

fifty _____

sixty _____

seventy _____

eighty _____

ninety _____

one hundred _____

Colors

black _____

red _____

brown _____

yellow _____

white _____

green _____

purple _____

orange _____

blue _____

silver _____

pink _____

gold _____

All Numbers to 100

1 one _____	26 twenty-six _____
2 two _____	27 twenty-seven _____
3 three _____	28 twenty-eight _____
4 four _____	29 twenty-nine _____
5 five _____	30 thirty _____
6 six _____	31 thirty-one _____
7 seven _____	32 thirty-two _____
8 eight _____	33 thirty-three _____
9 nine _____	34 thirty-four _____
10 ten _____	35 thirty-five _____
11 eleven _____	36 thirty-six _____
12 twelve _____	37 thirty-seven _____
13 thirteen _____	38 thirty-eight _____
14 fourteen _____	39 thirty-nine _____
15 fifteen _____	40 forty _____
16 sixteen _____	41 forty-one _____
17 seventeen _____	42 forty-two _____
18 eighteen _____	43 forty-three _____
19 nineteen _____	44 forty-four _____
20 twenty _____	45 forty-five _____
21 twenty-one _____	46 forty-six _____
22 twenty-two _____	47 forty-seven _____
23 twenty-three _____	48 forty-eight _____
24 twenty-four _____	49 forty-nine _____
25 twenty-five _____	50 fifty _____

51	fifty-one _____	76	seventy-six _____
52	fifty-two _____	77	seventy-seven _____
53	fifty-three _____	78	seventy-eight _____
54	fifty-four _____	79	seventy-nine _____
55	fifty-five _____	80	eighty _____
56	fifty-six _____	81	eighty-one _____
57	fifty-seven _____	82	eighty-two _____
58	fifty-eight _____	83	eighty-three _____
59	fifty-nine _____	84	eighty-four _____
60	sixty _____	85	eighty-five _____
61	sixty-one _____	86	eighty-six _____
62	sixty-two _____	87	eighty-seven _____
63	sixty-three _____	88	eighty-eight _____
64	sixty-four _____	89	eighty-nine _____
65	sixty-five _____	90	ninety _____
66	sixty-six _____	91	ninety-one _____
67	sixty-seven _____	92	ninety-two _____
68	sixty-eight _____	93	ninety-three _____
69	sixty-nine _____	94	ninety-four _____
70	seventy _____	95	ninety-five _____
71	seventy-one _____	96	ninety-six _____
72	seventy-two _____	97	ninety-seven _____
73	seventy-three _____	98	ninety-eight _____
74	seventy-four _____	99	ninety-nine _____
75	seventy-five _____	100	one hundred _____

U. S. Currency

a penny _____

a nickel _____

a dime _____

a quarter _____

a half dollar _____

a dollar _____

one cent _____

five cents _____

ten cents _____

twenty-five cents _____

fifty cents _____

one hundred cents _____

Time

1:00 _____

3:00 _____

6:00 _____

8:00 _____

9:30 _____

11:30 _____

Days

Monday _____

Tuesday _____

Wednesday _____

Thursday _____

Friday _____

Saturday _____

Sunday _____

yesterday _____

today _____

tomorrow _____

the day before yesterday_____

the day after tomorrow _____

Months

January _____

February _____

March _____

April _____

May _____

June _____

July _____

August _____

September _____

October _____

November _____

December _____

calendar _____

last month _____

this month _____

next month _____

the month before last _____

the month after next _____

Note to the teacher: Teach this vocabulary and the forms of *to be* with a calendar: Today is Monday; yesterday was Sunday; tomorrow will be Tuesday; this month is September; next month will be October, and so on.

Alphabet A–H

A, a _____

B, b _____

C, c _____

D, d _____

E, e _____

F, f _____

G, g _____

H, h _____

Note to the teacher: While students are still in the silent period, have them point to, write, or type letters as you say them. When they begin to speak, have them spell orally. At first allow them to see the word as they spell it. For students who are still struggling with letter names after your class begins reading, show words and alternately ask "How do you say it?" and "How do you spell it?"

Alphabet I–P

I, i _____

J, j _____

K, k _____

L, l _____

M, m _____

N, n _____

O, o _____

P, p _____

Alphabet Q–Z

Q, q _____

R, r _____

S, s _____

T, t _____

U, u _____

V, v _____

W, w _____

X, x _____

Y, y _____

Z, z _____

Classroom Nouns

a classroom _____

the teacher _____

students _____

the teacher's desk _____

the students' desks _____

John's desk _____

Ann's desk _____

the chalkboard _____

an eraser _____

a pencil sharpener _____

a waste paper basket _____

a book shelf _____

a bulletin board _____

Classroom Verbs

read _____

listen _____

write _____

open a book _____

close a backpack _____

clean a desk _____

Large Numbers: Hundreds and Thousands

one hundred _____

two hundred _____

three hundred _____

four hundred _____

five hundred _____

six hundred _____

seven hundred _____

eight hundred _____

nine hundred _____

one thousand _____

two thousand _____

three thousand _____

four thousand _____

five thousand _____

six thousand _____

seven thousand _____

eight thousand _____

nine thousand _____

ten thousand _____

twenty thousand _____

one hundred thousand _____

Arithmetic I: Addition and Subtraction

plus _____

minus _____

equals _____

3 + 1 _____

7 + 5 _____

2 + 0 _____

9 + 3 _____

8 + 6 _____

3 - 1 _____

7 - 5 _____

2 - 0 _____

9 - 3 _____

8 - 6 _____

Note to the teacher: If your students are mainstreamed into a math class, you can coordinate with the math teacher to help your students learn the vocabulary that matches the math concepts they are studying.

Arithmetic II: Multiplication and Division

times _____

divided by _____

7×8 _____

9×3 _____

5×8 _____

6×7 _____

12×4 _____

$9 \div 3$ _____

$48 \div 6$ _____

$81 \div 9$ _____

School Supplies

a tablet _____

scissors _____

a pencil _____

a pen _____

crayons _____

colored pencils _____

a red pencil, a green pencil, etc. _____

paste _____

construction paper _____

a pencil box _____

a spiral notebook _____

textbooks _____

a calculator _____

an automatic pencil _____

an eraser _____

a briefcase _____

Computer Nouns

a computer _____

a monitor _____

a screen _____

a mouse _____

mouse buttons _____

the keyboard _____

letter keys _____

the enter key _____

the space bar _____

arrows _____

arrow keys _____

the up arrow _____

the down arrow _____

the right arrow _____

the left arrow _____

a floppy disk _____

the floppy disk drive _____

a CD-ROM _____

the CD-ROM drive _____

speakers _____

a microphone _____

the printer _____

Computer Verbs

type _____

press a key _____

press the space bar _____

use the mouse _____

point _____

click _____

turn on the computer _____

insert a floppy _____

put in a CD _____

print _____

scan _____

Human Body/Possessive Nouns

fingers _____

hips _____

legs _____

feet _____

toes _____

Gary's head _____

Gary's face _____

Gary's eyes _____

Gary's ears _____

Gary's nose _____

Gary's chin _____

Gary's mouth _____

Gary's eyebrows _____

Gary's hair _____

Ann's torso _____

Ann's neck _____

Ann's shoulders _____

Ann's arms _____

Ann's elbows _____

Ann's hands _____

Note to the teacher: Use your students' names.

Family

a family _____

a woman _____

a man _____

a boy _____

a girl _____

a teenager _____

a baby _____

pets _____

a dog _____

a cat _____

husband _____

wife _____

brother _____

sister _____

father _____

son _____

mother _____

daughter _____

parents _____

children _____

Home Nouns

(A doll house works very well when teaching this vocabulary.)

a house _____

the living room _____

a bedroom _____

a bathroom _____

the big bathroom _____

the small bathroom _____

the kitchen _____

the dining room _____

the halls _____

the garage _____

Living Room

the living room _____

a coffee table _____

a sofa _____

a recliner _____

an armchair _____

a bookcase _____

a television _____

Bedroom

a bed _____

a pillow _____

blankets _____

a dresser _____

a lamp _____

Dining Room

the dining room _____

the table _____

chairs _____

plates _____

glasses _____

a pitcher _____

silverware _____

a fork _____

a spoon _____

a knife _____

Kitchen

the kitchen _____

the stove _____

the refrigerator _____

the sink _____

an electric mixer _____

a coffee pot _____

a knife _____

knives _____

tongs _____

Bathroom

a bathroom _____

a sink _____

the shower _____

the bathtub _____

the toilet _____

a mirror _____

the medicine cabinet _____

a towel _____

a washcloth _____

Home Verbs

sleep _____

watch television _____

laugh _____

cry _____

purr _____

pet the cat _____

dial the telephone _____

talk _____

fight _____

Park and Playground

the park _____

the picnic area _____

the playground _____

a picnic table _____

a picnic basket _____

a trash barrel _____

a grill _____

a cooler _____

a slide _____

a swing _____

a seesaw _____

a merry-go-round _____

monkey bars _____

Note to the teacher: This vocabulary is best taught at a park or on the school playground.

Pets and Pet Accessories

a dog _____

a leash _____

a doghouse _____

a cat _____

a litter box _____

a fish _____

a fishbowl _____

a bird _____

a cage _____

a hamster _____

a treadmill _____

Note to the teacher: If possible, bring the pets and accessories to class. If not, stuffed animals work well.

Farm Animals

a cow _____

a bull _____

a calf _____

cattle _____

a pig _____

a horse _____

a sheep _____

a goat _____

Wild Animals

a lion _____

a tiger _____

an elephant _____

a hippopotamus _____

a bat _____

a snake _____

an alligator _____

a giraffe _____

a deer _____

a lizard _____

a bird _____

Note to the teacher: Plush animals work very well for this vocabulary.

World Geography: Continents and Countries

Continents

maps _____

the world _____

North America _____

South America _____

Europe _____

Asia _____

Africa _____

Australia _____

Antarctica _____

Countries

(Include the home countries of all of your students.)

Canada _____

Mexico _____

the United States _____

Venezuela _____

China _____

Colombia _____

Brazil _____

Argentina _____

Chile _____

the Philippines _____

France _____

Great Britain _____

Note to the teacher: If students know enough geography to locate these places on a map, and if many English place names are cognates in their native language, introduce this vocabulary early. Otherwise, wait until later in the course.

U. S. Geography: Oceans, Rivers, Mountain Ranges, Borders

a map of the United States _____

the Pacific Ocean _____

the Pacific Coast _____

the Atlantic Ocean _____

the Atlantic Coast _____

the Gulf of Mexico _____

the Gulf Coast _____

the Mississippi River _____

the Great Lakes _____

the Rocky Mountains _____

the Appalachian Mountains _____

the Canadian border _____

the Mexican border _____

Ordinal Numbers

1st first _____

2nd second _____

3rd third _____

4th fourth _____

5th fifth _____

6th sixth _____

7th seventh _____

8th eighth _____

9th ninth _____

10th tenth _____

11th eleventh _____

12th twelfth _____

City Geography: Streets, Avenues, Buildings, Directions, Travel

1st Street _____

2nd Street _____

3rd Street _____

4th Street _____

5th Street _____

6th Street _____

7th Street _____

8th Street _____

9th Street _____

10th Street _____

11th Street _____

12th Street _____

A Avenue _____

B Avenue _____

C Avenue _____

D Avenue _____

E Avenue _____

F Avenue _____

G Avenue _____

H Avenue _____

I Avenue _____

J Avenue _____

K Avenue _____

L Avenue _____

library _____

bank _____

court house _____

park _____

church _____

bowling alley _____

high school _____

restaurant _____

shopping mall _____

shopping mall parking lot _____

gas station _____

grocery store _____

grocery store parking lot _____

bridge _____

Note to the teacher: Draw a map. At first, have students point to streets, avenues, and intersections. Later, have them say their names.

Fruits and Vegetables

Fruits

fruit _____

grapes _____

an apple _____

bananas _____

lemons _____

cherries _____

a pear _____

oranges _____

grapefruit _____

a pineapple _____

strawberries _____

raspberries _____

a peach _____

a papaya _____

Vegetables

lettuce _____

green beans _____

spinach _____

broccoli _____

radishes _____

peppers _____

a tomato _____

kidney beans _____

cauliflower _____

Note to the teacher: Toy food works well with this and the following vocabulary. Real food works even better, especially if the students are allowed to eat it. Gastrolinguistic lessons can, however, get expensive for those with large classes.

Meat and Seafood

meat _____

ground beef _____

steak _____

chicken _____

hot dogs _____

ribs _____

pork chops _____

seafood _____

fish _____

shrimp _____

lobster _____

oysters _____

crab _____

Bakery Products

loaves of bread _____

white bread _____

whole wheat bread _____

a cake _____

a cupcake _____

Danish pastry _____

a cinnamon roll _____

a doughnut _____

a bun _____

a pie _____

Dairy Products

milk _____

chocolate milk _____

cheese _____

cheddar cheese _____

Swiss cheese _____

cottage cheese _____

yogurt _____

butter _____

cream _____

ice cream _____

whipped cream _____

Note to the teacher: Ask students to categorize the various food items listed here. "Is a banana a fruit or a vegetable?" "Is cheese a bakery product or a dairy product?" "Are hot dogs seafood?" "Show me a bakery product." "Pick up and eat a fruit."

Women's Clothing

a sweater _____

a skirt _____

a dress _____

shoes _____

a hat _____

a blouse _____

jeans _____

a sweatshirt _____

sweatpants _____

tennis shoes _____

a T-shirt _____

shorts _____

socks _____

Men's Clothing

a shirt _____

slacks _____

a belt _____

a tie _____

a sports coat _____

shoes _____

gloves _____

a raincoat _____

boots _____

Expressing Emotions

smiling _____

frowning _____

jumping _____

shouting _____

kissing _____

yawning _____

sighing _____

crying _____

happy _____

sad _____

angry _____

in love _____

bored _____

excited _____

homesick _____

hungry _____

Note to the teacher: When students become more advanced, use these vocabulary words to teach complex sentences with *because*. "He is smiling because he is happy." "She is shouting because she is angry." "They are jumping and shouting because they are excited."

Baseball

a baseball _____

a glove _____

a bat _____

the bench _____

first base _____

second base _____

third base _____

home plate _____

outfield _____

pitcher _____

catcher _____

batter _____

outfielders _____

infielders _____

throwing _____

catching _____

hitting _____

running _____

waiting _____

Note to the teacher: If your school has a baseball diamond, teach this vocabulary there, or use an arcade-style computer baseball game. If your students prefer other sports, begin with them instead.

Possessive Pronouns

Gary and his wife _____

Ann and her husband _____

Gary and his children _____

Ann and her children _____

Ann and her sons _____

Gary and his daughters _____

Mandy and her parents _____

Mandy and her mother _____

Mandy and her father _____

Rick and his parents _____

Rick and his father _____

Rick and his mother _____

Bob and his sisters _____

Bob and his brother _____

Susan and her brothers _____

Susan and her sister _____

Mandy and her sister _____

Mandy and her brothers _____

Rick and his sisters _____

Rick and his brother _____

Susan and her pet _____

Rick and his pet _____

Fluffy and her master _____

Fido and his master _____

John and his book _____

Sue and her briefcase _____

Fulano and his pencils _____

Mai and her pen _____

Note to the teacher: Substitute names of students, teachers, and members of their families. Use your students' family pictures if possible.

Prepositions and Their Objects

a box _____

a basket _____

a glass _____

a table _____

a desk _____

a chair _____

a pencil _____

a ruler _____

a picture _____

a book, a ball _____

a cassette _____

a box on a table _____

a ball in a box _____

a chair by a desk _____

a pen under a table _____

a cassette in a desk _____

an eraser on a chair _____

a ruler by a ball _____

a pencil under a ruler _____

a ruler on a book _____

a box under a chair _____

a cassette by an eraser _____

a pencil between two books _____

a chair in front of a desk _____

a chair behind a table _____

a ball in front of a bookcase _____

a sofa between two chairs _____

a ruler behind a book _____

a pen between two pencils _____

an eraser in front of a ruler _____

a cassette behind a book _____

a box between two balls _____

a chair behind a bookcase _____

a pen in front of a box _____

a table in front of a sofa _____

a cassette between two rulers _____

a ball behind a box _____

Appendix 2

Recommended Sources

Recommended Reading

Asher, J. J. (2000). *Learning another language through actions.* Los Gatos, CA: Sky Oaks Productions.

Benedict, R. (1946/1989). *The chrysanthemum and the sword: Patterns of Japanese culture.* Boston: Houghton Mifflin.

Brown, H. D. (2000). *Principles of language learning and teaching* (4th ed.). White Plains, NY: Addison-Wesley, Longman.

Celce-Murcia, M. (2001). *Teaching English as a second or foreign language.* Boston, MA: Heinle.

Graham, C. (1979). *Jazz chants for children.* New York: Oxford University Press.

Donovan, S., & Cross, C. (2002). *Minority students in special and gifted education.* Washington, DC: National Academy Press.

Echevarria, J., & Graves, A. (1997). *Sheltered content instruction.* Boston: Allyn & Bacon.

Harley, B., Allen, P., Cummins, J., & Swain, M. (1990). *The development of second language proficiency.* New York: Cambridge University Press.

Kelly, L. G. (1976). *25 centuries of language teaching.* Rowley, MA: Newbury House Publishers.

Krashen, S. D., & Terrell, T. D. (1996). *The natural approach: Language acquisition in the classroom* (Rev. ed.). Englewood Cliffs, NJ: Prentice Hall.

Larsen-Freeman, D. (2000). *Techniques and principles in language teaching.* New York: Oxford University Press

O'Malley, J. M., & Valdez Pierce, L. (1996). *Authentic assessment for English language learners.* White Plains, NY: Addison-Wesley, Longman.

Parnwell, E. C. (1988). *The new Oxford English dictionary.* New York: Oxford University Press.

Podhaizer, M. E. (1998). *Painless spelling.* Hauppague, NY: Barrons Educational Series.

Shapiro, N., & Adelson-Goldstein, J. (1998). *The Oxford picture dictionary.* New York: Oxford University Press.

Snow, M. A., & Britton, D. M. (1997). *Content-based classroom: Perspectives on integrating language and content.* White Plains, NY: Addison-Wesley, Longman.

Vos Savant, M. (2001). *The art of spelling.* New York: W. W. Norton.

Wright, P., & Wright, P. (1999). *Wrightslaw: Special education law.* Hartfield, VA: Harbor House Law Press.

Recommended Web Sites

Dave's ESL Café   www.Eslcafe.com

This site claims that it is the Internet's meeting place for ESL/EFL students and teachers from around the world. It also boasts more than 1 million hits per month. It has great chat rooms and many useful links. It also has a great international job board for those who would like to try teaching ESL abroad.

The Linguistic Funland   www.tesol.net

This site provides links for teachers and students. One very special feature of Linguistic Funland is that it provides links to online student projects.

Karin's ESL Partyland   www.Eslpartyland.com

This site offers quizzes, forums, interactive lessons, and chat rooms for both ESL students and teachers. For teachers, Partyland also offers lesson plans and reproducible material to use in class.

WEB SITES THAT OFFER FREE E-BOOKS

The following Web sites offer both fiction and nonfiction public-domain books that can be downloaded or read online free of charge. Many English learners find that ebooks and dictionary software make reading faster and easier. Learners can even download some books in both English and their native language and use the native-language text to get through those sections of text that they do not understand in English.

Project Gutenberg	http://www.Promo.net/pg
Globusz Publishing	http://www.Globusz.com
Internet Public Library	http://www.Ipl.org

Recommended Periodicals

English Teaching Forum

This quarterly is published by the U. S. Department of State principally for American English teachers living abroad and is distributed through U.S. embassies. It is available in the United States and contains much of interest for stateside English teachers as well.

Room 304 (for submissions or letters to the editor) or Room 312 (for subscriptions)

301 4th Street, SW

Washington, DC 20547

Essential Teacher and TESOL Quarterly

Journals available to members of TESOL.

Teachers of English to Speakers of Other Languages, Inc

700 S. Washington St.

Suite 200

Alexandria, VA 22314-4287

www.tesol.org

Index

**CORWIN
PRESS**

The Corwin Press logo—a raven striding across an open book—represents the union of courage and learning. Corwin Press is committed to improving education for all learners by publishing books and other professional development resources for those serving the field of K-12 education. By providing practical, hands-on materials, Corwin Press continues to carry out the promise of its motto: **"Helping Educators Do Their Work Better."**